THE FACTORY GIRLS

THE FACTORY GIRLS

A Kaleidoscopic Account of the

Triangle Shirtwaist Factory Fire

BY CHRISTINE SEIFERT

**ZEST
BOOKS**

TABLE OF CONTENTS

7 ... **PROLOGUE**

12 ... CHAPTER 1

FIVE BRAVE GIRLS

24 ... CHAPTER 2

A PUFF OF SMOKE

38 ... CHAPTER 3

THE PRICE OF FASHION

55 ... CHAPTER 4

COMING TO AMERICA

71 ... CHAPTER 5

THE SELF-MADE MAN

78 ... CHAPTER 6

LIFE IN THE FACTORY

Connect with Zest!

- zestbooks.net/blog
- zestbooks.net/contests
- twitter.com/zestbooks
- facebook.com/BooksWithATwist

2443 Fillmore Street, Suite 340, San Francisco, CA 94115 | www.zestbooks.net

93 ... CHAPTER 7

CORRUPTION IN THE GILDED AGE

101 ... CHAPTER 8

UNION GIRLS

113 ... CHAPTER 9

TRIANGLE FACTORY ON STRIKE

129 ... CHAPTER 10

AFTER THE FLAMES

157 ... CHAPTER 11

HISTORY REPEATS

166 ... FOR FURTHER READING

168 ... SELECTED REFERENCES

Manufactured in the U.S.A. | 4500649165 | DOC 10 9 8 7 6 5 4 3 2 1

PROLOGUE

The Triangle Shirtwaist Factory fire of 1911 remains one of the worst workplace tragedies in American history. I first read about the fire my freshman year in college. I vividly remember sitting in the dining hall at lunch, opening my history textbook, and quickly becoming too absorbed in the story to eat my turkey sandwich. The book included only a couple of paragraphs—just a few measly lines to set up a longer section about labor policy in the Progressive Era. But I was desperate to know more: Who were these girls, and how did they end up in that New York City factory on March 25, 1911? What must life have been like for a factory girl in the early 1900s in America? And how do we make sure the factory girls' story is never forgotten? This book is an attempt to answer those questions.

But first, a few notes about how I went about researching this story. There is, fortunately for us, a rich array of primary and secondary sources that provide insight into the lives of the girls who worked in the Triangle Shirtwaist Factory. All the information in this book comes from multiple primary and secondary sources. (You'll find a complete reference section and suggestions for further reading at the end.) I, like anyone else who has written about the Triangle fire, am indebted to Leon Stein in particular. His 1985 book, *The Triangle Fire*, is a gold mine of primary source accounts, including oral histories. His work also informed an unparalleled online repository at Cornell University: http://trianglefire.ilr.cornell.edu/index.html. This website is a fantastic resource for anyone seeking to learn more about the Triangle tragedy. All the information I present that is directly related to the fire itself comes from Stein's book and the Cornell site. In some cases, I relied on books published after Stein's, including David von Drehle's *Triangle: The Fire That Changed America* (2003) and Albert Marrin's *Flesh and Blood So Cheap: The Triangle Fire and Its Legacy* (2011). These materials were critically important for my understanding of the fire, its victims, and the aftermath.

When sources disagreed, I generally went with Leon Stein's facts, except in cases where he was drawing from newspaper accounts. As von Drehle warns, newspaper reporting was often unreliable; publishers were eager to get stories out before reporters had proper and sufficient information. You'll find that, whenever necessary, I specify if a disagreement among sources stemmed from bad reporting.

Even with all the useful resources about the fire, details about the victims were often hard to find. Cornell's site was useful for biographical information. I also relied heavily on Ancestry.com and Ellis Island's immigration records. If I could, I would write the story of every girl in the factory, but biographical information is very hard to find, and in some cases the task is impossible. When I was able to access biographical information, I tried to paint as clear an image of the girl's life and background as I possibly could. In instances where I couldn't be sure about specific facts of day-to-day life, I indicate that I am hypothesizing based on historical research.

This book presents the story of five Triangle Factory workers: Annie Miller, Bessie Gabrilowich, Rose Rosenfeld, Fannie Lansner, and Kate Leone. You'll meet them in Chapter 1, where you'll learn about their families and their backgrounds. You'll also see exactly where they were in the factory that afternoon the fire broke out.

In Chapters 2 and 3, we'll leave our heroines for a bit to learn about what was happening in America that led to the expansion of factory-produced consumer goods. We'll start in the late 1800s to learn about the rise of consumerism and marketing, both of which led to mass production in the early 1900s. In Chapter 4, we'll look at immigration patterns in the later 1800s and early 1900s to understand why people were rushing to America at this particular time in history. In Chapter 5, we'll learn about the political and cultural climate then and how it foreshadowed troubling economic inequities, and why, as a result, labor unions formed to fight against unfair wages and unsafe working conditions. In Chapter 6, you'll discover what a day in the factories was like. Chapter 7 explores the extent of corruption in the Gilded Age and beyond that led to the factory conditions. In Chapters 8 and 9, you'll read about people who formed unions and fought against unfair labor practices.

In each chapter, you'll meet girls from all walks of life—girls who worked in factories, who married millionaires, and who led labor strikes. These vignettes are designed to give you a full picture of America at a pivotal moment in history. Most authors who have written about the Triangle fire focus on the progressive reforms prompted by the fire. While I'll certainly mention some of those reforms in workplace safety and pay equity, my goal is to present a thorough understanding of how culture, politics, labor policy, and economics came together to form conditions in which the Triangle fire was bound to happen. To do that, I refer back to the Gilded Age, a historical period that began around 1870 and lasted until about 1900. I spend a great deal of time exploring the Gilded Age to show you that the decisions that Americans made—about what they wore and how they bought it—slowly created conditions that culminated in the Triangle fire.

In Chapter 10, we'll return to our five heroines—Annie, Bessie, Rose, Fannie, and Kate—to learn what happened to them in the fire. Some survived; others did not. We'll reflect on their legacies and the ways they impacted the larger world that surrounded them.

As you'll see in Chapter 11, while American laws exist now to protect workers, companies often move their production offshore, where conditions are every bit as dire as those in early twentieth-century American factories. You'll read about some small ways you can help change the world by fighting against economic and labor policies that exploit workers in order to line the pockets of a few oligarchic companies. In some cases, you can make changes just by being more aware of your power as a consumer!

As you read, you might wonder why I often chose to call the young Triangle workers girls rather than women. That's because I want to underscore the point that, for the most part, the people involved were still children. Many weren't even teenagers yet. Even those who might be classified as women were heartbreakingly young. The term "girl" isn't meant to undermine any of the Triangle workers; instead, it is intended to recognize that the people most affected by the Triangle tragedy were very young—and that that was just one of the ways in which they were vulnerable.

As you can probably tell by now, this book, at its core, is about more than just that horrible day of the Triangle fire. It's about the days leading up to the fire, the days when America was changing in ways that would shape our nation into what it is today. It's the story of what happened after the fire, when survivors were forced to relive the pain in a trial that captivated the country. This book is also about the ways that our habits as consumers—then and now—shape the workplace and our labor force. It's about how the everyday decisions we make affect millions of other people—here at home and abroad, right now and in the future.

Most of all, let's not forget that this book is about the Triangle Factory workers, the victims of an economic and labor system that succeeded precisely because it exploited and sometimes destroyed the very workers that sustained the system. This is a book about people who deserve to be remembered: the girls.

CHAPTER 1
FIVE BRAVE GIRLS

The day's work was supposed to end at six in the afternoon. But, during most of the year we youngsters worked overtime until 9 p.m. every night except Fridays and Saturdays. No, we did not get additional pay for overtime. At this point it is worth recording the generocity [sic] of the Triangle Waist Co. by giving us a piece of apple pie for supper instead of additional pay!

—Pauline Newman

I longed for my mother and a home where it would be light and warm and she would be waiting when we came from work.

—Rose Cohen

On a Saturday afternoon in March 1911, a small fire started on the eighth floor of the ten-story Asch Building. The Triangle Shirtwaist Factory, at the intersection of Washington Place and Green Street in Manhattan, used the top three floors for its massive production of shirtwaists, a new kind of fashionable blouse that women all over America wanted to wear. The demand for shirtwaists was so high that the Triangle Factory employed more than five hundred workers who spent more than nine hours a day, six days a week, mass-producing garments for women of all ages and backgrounds.

The tiny fire that afternoon grew into a raging inferno, an uncontrollable fire that injured or killed hundreds of people. Those who survived were haunted for the rest of their lives by the images they saw, the sounds they heard, and the searing heat they felt. The Triangle Factory fire of 1911 is inarguably one of the greatest workplace tragedies in American history, and one that should never be forgotten.

The hundreds of young people working in the factory were mostly immigrants, often heartbreakingly young, almost all women, and all poor. The complete lack of regard shown for them by their employers and by the government (which had yet to regulate safety in workplaces) left them vulnerable. They trusted that they were safe when they went to work, but they were far from safe. In just fifteen terrifying minutes, almost 150 souls perished as a result of the flames or smoke inhalation, or the plummet to the sidewalk below.

As in many tragedies, a silver lining emerged, one that certainly wouldn't bring back the lives of these vibrant young people but would eventually change America. The Triangle fire eventually led to significant reforms in American workplace safety and labor laws

In this chapter, you'll meet five girls, ranging in age from fourteen to twenty-one, who were in the Triangle Factory on that fateful day. Some will survive. Some won't. All had dreams—dreams that didn't involve toiling in a factory for the rest of their lives.

ANNIE MILLER (16), THE FIGHTER

When Annie Miller made her way to work on Saturday, March 25, 1911, it was a day like any other day—save for Sunday, when she rested. The daughter of Austrian immigrants, Annie was born in America, the first American-born citizen in her family, and grew up in a small apartment on 154 Attorney Street, in Manhattan's Lower East Side. She lived with her parents, Adolph and Bessie Miller, and her two brothers. It wasn't a nice apartment by any stretch of the imagination, not even at the time, but it was home to the family, who had left Europe for new opportunities in a new country. (Today, a one-bedroom, eight-hundred-square-foot condo on Attorney Street sells for more than a million dollars. But Annie and her family certainly didn't have granite countertops, a rooftop garden, or access to exercise rooms that tenants there do now.) The location of the apartment was perfect for the Millers. The Triangle Factory was a little more than a mile away, so Annie could walk to work in just twenty minutes. Even on March 25, when the morning weather was wet, there was a chance for her to get some fresh air on her trek through the city to work.

To pay the bills, every member of the family had to work. While Annie probably would have loved to attend school, education was a luxury that most immigrant families couldn't afford. Annie, like most of the neighborhood girls her age, had a factory job that helped support her family and likely provided a few leftover pennies for herself. If she saved for a few months, she could buy a new hat, a pair of gloves, or a new blouse.

Some weeks Annie might have had enough to go to the movie theater. A ticket for short films would have been just a quarter or even less. Two days before the fire, a new short film had come out, one that Annie might have been looking forward to seeing after work. Called *The Lonedale Operator*, it was the thrilling drama about a young girl who has to deal with two robbers after agreeing to cover for her sick father at the Lonedale train station office. The girl proves cleverer than the villains bargain for. She locks herself in a room with the money and turns down the lights. When the men finally break in, they find her pointing a gun at them. They freeze until her boyfriend, the train operator, returns to the station. The big twist is that the girl's "gun" is no more than a monkey wrench. The heroine was played by Blanche Sweet, a movie star who in 1911 was just a year younger than Annie Miller. But Blanche Sweet's life was surely far more exciting than Annie's. Faced with boring and repetitive work all day long, Annie must have relished the adventure and romance—and teenage heroines—that were available to her (almost exclusively) at the movies.

By our standards today, Annie's factory job wasn't a good job. It was hard labor. Annie had to work six days a week for nine or more hours a day—sometimes as many as fourteen hours a day. She was given very few breaks, including just a short period for eating her lunch. She wasn't allowed to talk with her coworkers while she was working. That would've slowed everybody down, and productivity was paramount.

To add insult to injury, Annie and her colleagues were searched on their way out of the building to make sure they hadn't stolen anything. The owners of garment factories feared that the young girls they employed would be tempted to steal a bit of a ribbon or a piece of material if given the chance.

For all her hard work and the sacrifice of her education, Annie probably made no more than about $6 a month. But getting a job at the Triangle Shirtwaist Factory was quite an accomplishment. At the age of sixteen, Annie had a few years to go before getting married, which meant that she still had time to move up the ladder in the factory—something that was made more likely by the fact that she was American born. She might one day become a forewoman and increase her monthly pay. That job was at least less boring and offered more opportunity for a girl to use her brain.

A few minutes after 4:30 on that Saturday afternoon, Annie was wrapping up her workday. She gathered her coat, her hat, and her pocketbook. She would have been walking briskly, a spring in her step, because she didn't have to return to the factory until Monday morning. It wasn't much of a weekend, but it was something. All the girls looked forward to quitting time on Saturday. Even though they were bone tired, they made the most of their free evenings.

As Annie made her way to the stairs at quitting time, she must have smelled smoke. She might have felt the panic start to rise as one or two people yelled, "Fire!" She would have been among the swarm of movement as everyone ran for one of the two exits. The Greene Street exit was already engulfed in flames. Those who made it to those doors were stuck anyway because they pressed their bodies against the door and were unable to open it inward. The Washington Place exit was locked, as always, to ensure that all workers could be checked for theft on their way out. Annie was lucky because she didn't head for either exit. She made it into one of the elevators almost immediately. (There were two freight elevators and two passenger elevators.)

Once the elevator doors opened on the first floor, she ran out into the fresh air and stood outside, with the flames shooting from the building above her. She would have felt the heat even out there on the sidewalk. Not far away, in Washington Square Park, she would have heard the sounds of children playing on a spring day.

What happened next is hard to imagine. Most of us would have been too traumatized to move and too scared to worry about our friends. We might have stood outside the building in a state of disbelief or even panic as we waited for the fire truck to show up. Indeed, passersby did line up outside the factory and watch as flames lit up the building, horrified, and unsure what to do.

Annie was not like the bystanders. She didn't panic. She didn't freeze in terror. Instead, she thought about two of her coworkers, immigrant girls who sat next to her at her worktable. She realized she hadn't seen them get up and leave when she had. She hadn't spotted them in the elevator either. And she didn't see them outside. Without a thought for her own safety, Annie ran back into the building.

As girls were pouring out of the elevator, Annie was the lone figure going back inside the smoky car. She rode up to her floor and, by some miracle, found those two immigrant girls. They were confused and in a state of panic. Annie calmly led them back to the elevator. They waited until the car arrived and Annie pushed both girls inside. She intended to follow them, but something happened. Annie tripped, or she was pushed in the crowd. She fell in front of the elevator, and as she struggled to get up, girls trampled over her. Annie would have covered her head and crawled below the smoke to find a place on the floor where she had room to move.

When she found a free space, Annie pushed herself to her feet. But the elevator was gone. Annie didn't know this, but that was the last time the elevator would descend before flames began nipping at her feet. All she knew at the moment was that the flames were getting closer and she didn't have time to wait for the elevator to unload and return. She did the only thing she could with fire at her heels: She ran to the window.

BESSIE GABRILOWICH (19), THE BIG SISTER

Israel Yonkel Gabrilowich was a busy man. He had ten children through three marriages (not all at the same time, of course). After the death of his first two wives, Israel married Meri Hinde. Together they had two daughters, Bessie and Pauline. Bessie had dark, curly hair and an adorable button nose. She had a friendly look about her, one that showed her kindness and compassion.

Bessie and her family had emigrated from Russia to the United States for a new life and more opportunity. They were from a city called Navahrudak, a very beautiful and old city in present-day Belarus, dating back to the thirteenth century. As Jews in Russia, they had faced unspeakable persecution and constant threats to their livelihood and personal safety. So they had saved up for tickets on a steamship and eventually settled in New York, where Bessie took a job at the Triangle Shirtwaist Factory, just like thousands of other eastern European immigrant girls who were expected to help their families.

Being in America and having a job and a little bit of money gave Bessie opportunities she wouldn't have had in Russia. She could even buy a few things for herself every now and then, but she couldn't spend too much. She was helping her family save enough money to bring her half-sisters—still in Russia—to New York.

The Triangle Factory seemed like a good place to work. Bessie had many friends at the factory. She sat with them during short lunch breaks at the windowsills, where they could eat and chat and look out the windows. Bessie had once wondered aloud during one of those lunch breaks what would happen if there was ever a fire....

At 4:30 that Saturday, Bessie was celebrating the engagement of a ninth-floor coworker. Bessie was enjoying a piece of cake with her friends at the end of their nine-hour shift. She would have been tired, of course, but still happy for the chance to celebrate with a friend. Getting married wasn't a surefire ticket out of the factory, but it often did mean a step up in living conditions. Bessie's friend might have been lucky enough to be marrying someone with an education who could provide a better life for her. Bessie, like most of the factory girls, had little formal education, and her current prospects were largely confined within the walls of the factory.

During the engagement party, Bessie's young friend, Dora, complained to Bessie that she wasn't paid enough. Bessie had recently asked her boss for a raise and gotten it. She'd successfully raised her salary by two whole dollars a month, an increase she most certainly deserved. Bessie had been employed at the factory for two years and had worked her way into a position as a stitcher. Such a position required a certain amount of talent, and Bessie was very good at her job. She also had the guts to ask for a raise, something that a lot of girls simply didn't do because they were scared of being fired just for asking.

Bessie encouraged Dora to be brave and approach her boss before leaving for the day. So while Bessie finished her cake, Dora left—steely in her resolve—to talk to her boss. Bessie had a younger sister, so she probably felt protective of Dora. She wanted to help her any way she could, and she didn't think Dora should wait another day to ask for the salary she deserved.

Just as Bessie was teaching a coworker at the engagement party a new dance step, she heard someone yell, "Fire!" Unaware of how bad the flames had gotten already, she and the other workers left the party and went to the cloakroom to retrieve their coats, hats, and pocketbooks. Bessie wasn't about to leave behind her new spring straw hat, one she'd bought just the day before with her hard-earned money.

Outside the little cloakroom in the corner of the factory floor, her foreman stopped her. "Save yourself, Bessie!" he yelled to her in Yiddish. That's when Bessie realized how serious things were. She grabbed her things and turned around and headed to the main stairway where the girls exited the factory each day.

Since the main doors on the eighth and ninth floors were always kept locked as a measure against theft, the girls were used to lining up and having their bags searched as they left. Only then could they exit through the doors. That afternoon, Bessie either forgot about the locked doors or hoped someone had unlocked them, given the emergency. Either way, she must have been devastated when she discovered that the door wasn't moving.

While many girls panicked when they discovered the locked door, Bessie kept her cool. She put on her new hat, but she decided to leave her coat. She turned around and headed back to the stairs that ran alongside the freight elevator. She paused for a moment, probably to check on other girls. What she saw horrified her. Little Dora, the girl she had encouraged to ask for a raise, was standing at the window with a look of terror on her face. Bessie watched helplessly as other girls near Dora jumped out the window. When she turned back again, Dora was gone. She'd jumped. Dora might have been safely out of the building prior to the fire if Bessie had not told her to talk to the foreman.

As distraught as she was, Bessie didn't have time to think. Instead, she waited until the door was unlocked by someone with a key, covered her face with her purse to ease her breathing, and ran down ten flights of stairs, hoping she could outrun the flames and the smoke that was so thick that she could barely see in front of her. While she ran, she must have been thinking about sweet-faced Dora, her friend, who trusted and looked up to Bessie like her big sister.

ROSE ROSENFELD (17), THE THINKER

Rose Rosenfeld came to America from Austria with her parents. They had wanted to join Rose's brother, who'd already moved to America and had an impressive home. Unlike many immigrant families, the Rosenfelds were not dirt poor in Russia. They weren't rich either, but they were certainly not destitute. They came to America not because they were fleeing poverty but because they wanted a new life in a place where they wouldn't be persecuted for being Jewish.

Her brother had written to Rose that Americans "were working people." And Rose wanted nothing more than to fit in with them. "I want to show that I'm a real American," she said, "and I want to work like everybody else." Almost as soon as she stepped off the boat, she set off to find a job that would put money in her pocket.

Rose quickly found work on the ninth floor of the Triangle Shirtwaist Factory. It wasn't easy to be a factory girl, but Rose was smart and hardworking. And she had to have been well liked by her coworkers, what with her broad, friendly smile and her positive attitude.

On the morning of March 25, 1911, Rose was probably looking forward to her birthday, just two days away. She was going to turn eighteen years old. That Saturday morning she fixed her hair in the fashion of the day, parting it a bit off center and then pulling it back loosely before tying it with a bow. It may seem like a ridiculous hairstyle now, but Rose pulled it off because of her heart-shaped face and her pretty, bright eyes.

Like most of the girls on her floor of the factory that afternoon, Rose was gathering her things to leave for the day. She had much to look forward to that weekend. At 4:40 p.m. or so, she heard someone yell fire. By that time, the smoke was already filling the room.

Rose followed the rush of people to the closest door, which was firmly locked. The fire quickly grew, fueled by all the flammable material in the room. Fabrics were even draped across windows and the ceilings, making the room a boxed inferno. Rose knew she had to make a quick decision. She saw the other girls panicking, screaming, and pushing, desperate to get to the elevators or to the windows at the side of the room. She paused and asked herself: What would the executives be doing?

The executives were housed on the tenth floor, the top floor of the building, which meant they had roof access and could potentially get out that way. Bingo! Rose had figured out a solution. She ran for the open Greene Street stairs, before the flames got too high and blocked the door, and went up as everyone else on her floor fought to go down. She entered the smoky tenth floor to find it unsettlingly quiet. The floor was completely deserted because the executives had already left. They hadn't even thought to open the doors downstairs for the hundreds of people stuck in the building. Instead, as soon as someone reported the fire, the executives simply left through unlocked doors on the tenth floor, unobstructed stairways, or functioning elevators. What a sharp contrast to the situation on the floors below, where all the girls were essentially trapped.

Rose must have looked around that giant, empty space and realized right there that the factory executives didn't care enough about her or any of her colleagues to save them from a burning building. Here she was, alone on the top floor of a ten-story building, flames rising and smoke growing thicker by the second, and she had to make a choice: look for a way out on the tenth floor, or go back into the fire below to help the others?

FANNIE LANSNER (21), THE LEADER

Fannie Lansner arrived alone in the United States from Russia in 1904 when she was just fourteen years old. She boarded with the Finkelman family on Forsyth Street in Manhattan. Solomon Finkelman and his wife, also named Fannie, owned a shop. They also had a four-year-old son named David. Living with a family probably helped quell the homesickness Fannie felt. Imagine being in New York, thousands of miles from home, without any family nearby.

Like other immigrant girls, Fannie didn't go to school when she got to New York. Instead, she had to work in order to support herself. Unlike many immigrants, though, Fannie could read and write English, skills that would have given her a leg up in the factory. After a relatively short period, Fannie had become a forewoman on the ninth floor of the Triangle Factory.

She was a particularly beloved forewoman. Her girls—the workers she supervised—appreciated her kindness. If a girl was fired for some minor infraction, which unfortunately happened often, Fannie would talk to the bosses and put in a good word for the girl, and sometimes the girl would get her job back. Fannie was also unfailingly fair. She might have expected a lot of work from her girls, but she gave just as much herself. Girls had to work hard under Fannie's watch, and she put in the same work right alongside them.

On the day of the fire, Fannie was finishing her workday along with her girls. When someone yelled fire and the girls began to panic, she remained calm. She had to. She was the forewoman, the leader. Her girls looked up to her, and she knew they needed her to keep it together. She immediately gathered the panicking girls and led them to the elevator car. She kept a small group of girls corralled near the elevator. While they were waiting for the car, she led other girls to the stairways and sent them down in an orderly fashion once the doors were unlocked. She calmed girls who were screaming and crying, hysterical with fear, and spoke to each of them as calmly as she could, using English and Yiddish to ensure that she was understood.

Fannie sent down group after group until the elevator stopped coming to the ninth floor. What she didn't know was that the girls below her on the eighth floor were getting the elevator first. In fact, the girls on the eighth floor were jumping on top of the car on its way down. And all that weight eventually slowed down the car. On the last trip from the ninth floor, the girls climbing aboard the elevator begged her to ride with them. She calmly told them that she would be "all right." She wouldn't leave until every last one of her girls was safely outside. Fannie could not have known that would be the last time the elevator stopped at her floor.

In spite of the chaos in the building, Fannie led hundreds of her girls to safety. Fannie was just that kind of person—a leader. When the elevator stopped coming, Fannie had to find a Plan B to save herself.

KATE LEONE (14), THE BABY

Kate Leone was among the youngest workers at the Triangle Factory. She was an Italian American beauty with a sly smile and heavy-lidded eyes. Like the other girls in the factory, she wore her dark hair pulled back and fluffed out in the style of the day.

Kate's parents, Vito (later known as Victor) Leone and Luisa Kischlin, emigrated from Germany and got married in 1887 in New York. Luisa gave birth to eight children, though sadly four of them died as infants.

As the eldest daughter, Kate was sent off to work rather than to school. She was pleased to get a job on the ninth floor of the Triangle Factory along with her older cousins, Michelina Nicolesei and Annie Colletti. Kate must have felt very grown up as she left for work each morning alongside her family members who were seven years older than she was. Here she was, earning a paycheck for her family and becoming an independent American girl.

On the afternoon of March 25, 1911, Kate was finishing her work-day. She'd only been at the factory for a few weeks. In that time, she'd made $3, a sum that must have felt like a fortune to her. Imagine how excited she would have been to collect that first paycheck, to come home to her family with money to contribute.

Like her older coworkers, she ran to the exit when the first cries rang out, and found it locked. Multiple girls pushed and pulled at the door, but no amount of force could budge that lock. Nobody knew where the keys might be, and the fire was spreading. Soon, Kate found herself in the middle of a pack of girls moving as a unit from the locked door to the elevator area. She might have been looking for her cousins, but she couldn't see them anywhere. Was that because they were already outside? Did they find another exit? She wanted to wait for them, but she knew she had to get out.

The smoke was so thick that it would have been hard to see. Kate had to move fast before the smoke filled her lungs.

CHAPTER 2

A PUFF OF SMOKE

While most of the garment manufacturing establishments in New York City are not any better as far as fire protection is concerned, it is significant that the worst calamity happened at the Triangle, known among the workpeople in the trade as the "prison." The name is probably due the extraordinary discipline with poor earning for which the firm is famous.

—Ladies' Garment Worker, April 1911

"Is it a man or a woman?" asked the reporter. "It's human, that's all you can tell," answered the policeman.'

—*The New York Times*, March 26, 1911

What actually happened before the girls knew to leave the building on March 25th? The story is surprisingly simple: Not long after 4:30 p.m., someone on the eighth floor discarded a still smoldering cigarette. That's it. One little cigarette sent an entire building up in flames.

Fire investigators would later recover multiple cigarette butts on the eighth floor, which indicated that smoking, though technically prohibited, was commonplace in the factory. The person smoking on this particular day was most likely a foreman at the end of his shift. He might have flicked the cigarette into a nearby ashtray or receptacle. What he didn't know was that the cigarette was still lit.

On the eighth floor alone, forty cutters, all men, worked at long tables. Alongside the cutters were a hundred women basters who, following paper patterns, made temporary stitches until the materials could be sewn permanently. While the women basted, the cutters worked through more than a hundred layers of fabric and sheer tissues patterns. Fabric scraps would fall to the floor and were stored beneath the tables. The lightweight cotton was filled with pockets of air, which also made the fabric highly flammable. Every other month, when two thousand pounds of fabric had accumulated, the factory would sell a pile of scraps to rag dealers who went all over the city buying up cloth that they would then resell to textile factories. At the time of the fire, the rag dealer hadn't been by since January. That meant there was close to a ton of flammable material on the floor alone!

The eighth floor was supervised by family members of the factory owners, Max Blanck and Isaac Harris. The manager of the eighth and ninth floor was Samuel Bernstein, whose sister Bertha was Blanck's wife and a cousin of Harris's wife, Bella. It was actually Harris's sister, Eva, one of the girls working on the eighth floor, who first noticed the fire. Samuel went to check it out, but he wasn't particularly worried. He'd seen fires on the floor before, and kept red fire buckets full of water at various points in the factory for exactly these kinds of episodes. But when Bernstein got to the fire he saw there was no time to waste: This was not a flickering spark; it was a full-fledged fire. He grabbed pails full of water and began dumping them over the flames. But he was no match for the hungry fire. Above the cutting tables were rows of hanging patterns made of a thin, flammable paper. The flames leapt high and latched onto the patterns, and before long, the whole room seemed to be on fire. As the flaming patterns fell, they ignited the fabric on the table as well. Soon the room was an inferno.

PRECIOUS MINUTES

The first three minutes of the fire were particularly confusing and chaotic. So much was happening at the same time that it's hard to get a complete picture of what exactly transpired inside the factory. What we do know is that Bernstein had precious little time to either warn the others or attempt to subdue the fire. As it turned out, the fire would consume the eighth floor in about five minutes. That's nine thousand square feet, about the same size as a baseball infield. His decision to spend even a couple of minutes on fighting the fire, as we will later see, had tragic repercussions.

Unable to quell the fire with the water from the buckets, Bernstein yelled for a shipping clerk, Louis Sederman, to get the fire hose. Sederman tried every hose and got nothing. There was no water pressure. According to one report, the hose had never been connected to the standpipe. (A standpipe is a vertical pipe that is connected to a water supply. A firefighter can then hook up the hose to that pipe and spray water on a fire. It's kind of like a fire hydrant.)

Bernstein climbed on top of the worktable and began dumping water over the fire. He was hoping that a different angle would help—but to no avail. The flames simply got bigger. Bernstein decided there was no way to put out the fire. They all needed to leave the building immediately. Yet workers still streamed to the dressing room to get their hats and coats. "For God's sake," Bernstein yelled, "get out of here as quick as you can!" Bernstein stayed, however, determined to get everyone out before he left the building.

Dinah Lipschitz, who kept ledgers for the Triangle Factory, was busy recording figures with a pencil and paper on the eighth floor when she heard the alert from Bernstein. She knew she needed to send an alert to the ninth and tenth floors. Rather than calling on the house phone, she made an odd decision: She used the telautograph.

Before fax machines, companies used a contraption called the telautograph. It was basically a pad of paper and pen connected by wire to another pad and pen in a different location. When the messenger wrote, the movement of her pen was supposed to be replicated at the other location. Lipschitz wrote "FIRE!" on her side, but the receiver on the tenth floor, Mary Alter, heard only the telautograph signal. No words appeared, so after a moment Alter went back to her work. She had a string of figures in mind that she didn't want to forget, not to mention that the switchboard operator had called in sick that day, which meant Alter had worked two jobs all day. Plus, she had never trusted the telautograph because it frequently did not work right. She was used to getting half messages or no message at all. She said, "I realized that it was a new machine and that a good many of the girls did not yet know how to operate it properly. They often made mistakes and didn't connect things right. So I went back to my desk thinking that someone was fooling me."

Lipschitz waited two minutes before she figured that Alter must not have received the message and then picked up the phone. She was understandably worked up, and it took a few seconds for Alter to interpret what she was saying. As soon as Alter heard the word fire, she dropped the phone and ran to tell the others on the tenth floor. Lipschitz was still on the phone and had no idea if Alter had the message, and to make matters worse, she couldn't call the ninth floor herself. The way the phone system was set up, any call to another floor had to go through the switchboard. By the time Alter finally got back to the phone and put Lipschitz through to the ninth floor, everyone there had already learned of the fire because they were seeing it with their own eyes.

In the meantime, Bernstein, who had given up on fighting the fire with water, tried to enter the ninth floor from the stairs, but the flames were already too big. He couldn't enter the room. He ran up another flight of stairs to the tenth floor where he found the company's managers and executives "running around like wildcats" as they scrambled to get out. So Bernstein made his way back to the eighth floor.

Meanwhile, at about 4:45 p.m., John Mooney, a bystander outside on the street, noticed the smoke from the building and pulled fire alarm No. 289 on Greene Street. Just seconds later someone inside the factory pulled a fire alarm. And someone else, probably Alter at the switchboard, phoned the fire department from the tenth floor. Almost immediately after those alerts, firemen in a horse-drawn carriage were on their way. The fire station was only six blocks away, just minutes by horse, but minutes were all it took for the fire to spread, especially on the eighth and ninth floors where all the paper and fabric were located.

Factory co-owner Isaac Harris was in his tenth-floor office on the phone with a salesman when he heard the sounds of panic. He hung up to investigate what was going on. Harris assumed he and others could easily put out the fire themselves. Just a couple of years before, he'd seen a fire in a scrap basket. He quickly moved the burning basket to another part of the factory floor where there were fewer people and poured water on it. That fire's culprit was in the bottom of the basket: a cigarette butt. Harris found and immediately fired the operator responsible for the smoking. Undoubtedly, when he realized there was another fire, he was ready to put it out just as he had the last time. Harris was likely on his way to have a look at the fire when he spotted flames through the windows on the tenth floor, the smoke blowing up from the floors below. It dawned on him then that this was far bigger than what he had encountered before.

Harris's co-owner, Blanck, was also on the tenth floor and was with his daughters, twelve-year-old Henrietta and five-year-old Mildred. The little girls been brought to the factory by their governess, and they were positively delighted by their father's promise to take them shopping after work. By all accounts—except Blanck's, that is—Blanck froze, unsure of what to do when he learned about the fire. The head of shipping, Eddie Markowitz, led Blanck to the stairs. Markowitz said, "I pulled him by the coat and I said, 'Come along, Mr. Blanck.'" Markowitz could feel the heat of the flames where they stood as he urged Blanck to leave the building. He probably saved Blanck's life, along with the lives of his little girls.

Harris, unlike Blanck, did not freeze. He began pushing people into the elevator as fast as he could. When the elevators stopped moving, Harris then led people to the stairs to the roof, where they were able to escape to the neighboring NYU building via a ladder set out by NYU students. He escaped that way as well.

SINGED AND SMOLDERING

Louis Brown, a machinist, came out of the eighth-floor bathroom just as people were starting to exit the building. He saw the out-of-control fire and searched for water, just as Bernstein had done, but Bernstein told him it was too late for water. Together, the two men started ushering girls to the stairs. One girl almost fainted, but Bernstein slapped her and told her to run. Another girl tried to go back for her purse, but Bernstein ordered her to keep moving forward.

Unfortunately, the first girls to reach the eighth-floor stairway door couldn't open it. So many of them had packed up against it that nobody could get the inward-swinging door to move. And even if they could, nobody in that crowd had a key.

Ida Cohen, one of the sewing machine operators on the eighth floor, was at the front of the group and closest to the door. Her face was smashed right up against the door itself. "All the girls was falling on me," she later reported. She pleaded, "Please girls, let me open the door." It was Brown, the person who had come out of the bathroom, who finally managed to push through the crowd. As a higher-level worker, Brown had a key, which he used to open the door, and then with all his strength, he moved the crowd back far enough to get the door to swing open. The stairway was narrow and dark. The girls had to rush blindly down the stairs, covering their mouths to avoid breathing in the smoke. Anyone who fell was trampled and either had to be helped up or had to fight her way back to her feet.

While Brown was opening the doors on the eighth floor, Bernstein worked as fast as he could to get everyone else on the elevators. He tried to make sure he hadn't forgotten anyone, but the smoke made it very hard to see. Lipschitz, brave as any of the men who stayed behind, was still at her phone doggedly trying to reach the ninth floor. Bernstein told her to leave. They both had relatives on the ninth floor, but there was nothing they could do to get to them. They simply had to hope that the trapped workers upstairs could find their own way out.

The eighth-floor crowds continued to surge toward the door and the elevators, but the cars quickly became too crowded as workers pushed to get inside. The passenger elevators were designed to hold only about a dozen people; in the panic, approximately two dozen people at a time were boarding each elevator. The elevator operator bravely made as many trips as he could, saving about 150 people.

Katie Weiner, a lace cutter, had only been working at the factory for about five months. She was among the last people waiting for the elevator. As she watched the fire grow from the eighth floor, something inside her knew the elevator wouldn't be coming back up. She just had a feeling. So she made a snap decision: As the elevator was descending, she jumped into the elevator shaft, landing on top of the other girls. "Girls," she pleaded, "my feet are being crushed!" That load did make it down, but the elevator eventually stopped operating when the heat of the fire bent the elevator tracks.

Those who didn't make it to the elevator or the stairway door tried the fire escape. Poorly constructed, the rickety structure only provided enough room for people to walk in single file. Even then, the fire escape began to bow as soon as more than a handful of people loaded onto it. As more girls climbed in, it began to shake. The entire fire escape collapsed before long. Those who were unlucky enough to be on the fire escape when it crumbled fell and landed eight stories below.

Before the fire escape collapsed, one clever girl at the front of the line decided to exit at the sixth floor, two floors below the fire. She made a wise choice. The fire escape didn't go all the way to the ground floor anyway, though she probably didn't know that at the time. When she went into the building at the sixth floor, a line of girls followed her. With a bare hand, she broke the sixth-floor window and led a group to a loft area. Officer James Meehan, one of the first policemen on the scene, had entered the building via the stairs and heard the girls pounding on the locked sixth-floor door. He put his back to the door and used his legs to bust it open. All the girls were able to walk to the first floor and exit safely.

LADDERS FROM HEAVEN

The women and girls who were still left on the tenth floor (without the aid of elevators to bring them down) climbed out the window and found help from an unlikely group of people: the young men in the building next door, owned by New York University (NYU). That afternoon, thirty students were sitting in a lecture given by NYU law professor Frank Sommer, previously the sheriff of Essex County in New Jersey. Professor Sommer was teaching his class when he looked up and saw smoke coming from the Asch Building. Ironically, Sommer's colleague, Professor Francis Aymar, had written a concerned letter just a month earlier to the New York City Building Department. From the NYU building, Professor Aymar could see just how bad the safety conditions were inside the factory. The Building Department promptly replied, saying the staff would check into the situation. Had the department done that and then required Harris and Blanck to make the factory floors safer, Professor Sommer would not have looked up to see a fire; instead, he would have seen the regular hustle and bustle of quitting time inside the building.

Nevertheless, Professor Sommer acted quickly and ordered his students to grab two ladders that painters had fortuitously left behind the day before. The boys followed orders and readied the ladders as quickly as they could. It must have felt like providence to find exactly what they needed to mount a rescue mission. By positioning the ladders between the buildings just so, the students created a rickety drawbridge across which people could crawl. Even though the NYU building was fifteen feet higher than the Asch Building, this makeshift NYU rescue squad was able to lift a number of people from the tenth floor to safety inside the NYU building. Some of those rescued had singed hair and burnt clothing, but all who made it across the ladder bridge walked down the stairs of the NYU building and outside to safety.

LIKE FLAMING ROCKETS

The ninth-floor workers didn't fare as well as their colleagues on the eighth and tenth floors. For one thing, the fire spread significantly faster on the ninth floor. Since the elevator was stopping and loading people only from the eighth floor, the wind gusted through the elevator shaft and blew embers from the fire into the air of the ninth floor, landing on the shirtwaist material. Nearby were cans of oil used to grease the sewing machines. Basically everything on the ninth floor was flammable. The conditions were ideal for a raging fire.

The ninth-floor layout was also problematic. Eight tables were spread out across the room from the Washington Place exit to the fire escape, blocking easy access. The chairs on either side of the tables were so close together that they were back to back. The tight quarters made it difficult for people to move quickly, especially with smoke and flames hindering visibility. On the tables were more than two hundred sewing machines, too; so even if someone jumped on top of the tables to get across the room—which some of the girls did—they would have to be able to navigate around the bulky machinery without tripping and falling.

Some of the ninth-floor workers made it out of the Greene Street stairway once it was unlocked, but in a matter of moments the flames made that exit unusable. The crowd who hadn't made it out in the first wave ran for the elevator. They waited and waited for the elevator doors to open, but the elevator simply never came to the ninth floor. Finally, some of the girls pried the doors open. Those who thought quickly grabbed the elevator cable and swung onto the top of the car, damaging their hands if they didn't happen to be wearing gloves. Some girls lost their grip and fell down the elevator shaft. Inside, the girls could hear the terrifying thump of bodies landing atop of the car. Joseph Zitto, the elevator operator, made multiple trips up and down, knowing that each time he arrived he might open the doors to the flames. At one point, he could see the elevator shaft filling with flames. When the car finally slipped down to the bottom of the shaft, Zitto looked back and saw the girls who didn't make it. "It was horrible," he said. "They kept coming down from the burning floors above. Some of their clothing was burning as they fell. I could see the streaks of fire coming down like flaming rockets."

Sadly, no one who ran to the Washington Place exit would be able to make it out alive. That door was securely locked, as it always was during the day. Most who went to that exit then turned to the windows, where there was no way out but down. By the time the girls recognized that fact, the fire had spread across the ninth floor, making it impossible to cross to another exit. It all came down to what side of the room a girl happened to be on when the fire broke out.

One of the lucky survivors was Rose Glantz. "We didn't have a chance," she later reported about the ninth-floor workers. "The people on the eighth floor must have seen the fire start and grow. The people on the tenth floor got the warning over the telephone. But with us on the ninth, all of a sudden the fire was all around." Glantz saved herself by wrapping her scarf around her head and running through flames to a stairwell that had been unlocked.

NINE STORIES UP

At the time of the fire, just down the street from the Asch Building, social worker Frances Perkins was having tea at a friend's apartment. Perkins worked with the Consumers' League, an organization dedicated to improving factory-working conditions. Alerted by the sound of the

Horse-drawn fire engines on their way to the fire.

fire engines, Perkins and her friend ran to Washington Square Park and looked on from the sidewalk outside of the building.

What they saw was a life-and-death drama in real-time. Girls inside the building broke the windows with their bare hands. They inhaled fresh air and stepped outside to the ledge and waited for the firefighters' ladders to reach them. There was only one problem: The ladders only made it up to the seventh floor. The girls were left with two options, neither of which were promising: go back into a burning building, or jump to a near certain death on the pavement below. Perkins never forgot what she saw on that sidewalk. From that day forward, she devoted her life to making changes to the American workplace. But those changes wouldn't help the girls who were stuck in the Triangle Factory right at that moment.

James Cooper, who happened to be passing by the Asch Building, saw what appeared to be a bundle falling from window. He described the bundle "like a bale of dark dress goods." Another passerby guessed that the owner was "trying to save the best cloth." Both men were shocked when the "bundles" turned out to be human beings.

Firemen quickly opened big nets to catch falling girls. Like raindrops, they fell from the sky as people on the street looked up. Passersby spread open blankets and coats because the girls kept coming, one after another, and the firemen simply didn't have enough nets. But even if they had enough, the nets and blankets couldn't hold the weight of a falling person. And so, one by one, the bodies stacked up on the sidewalk. The girls fell so fast in such quick succession that the firemen didn't even have time to cover the bodies. Horrified bystanders could do nothing but watch as the girls leapt.

"Don't jump!" the crowds yelled. "Wait!" A few more minutes, and maybe the firemen would have figured out a way to catch them. Maybe the fireman could have reached the girls with a longer ladder. Maybe one would turn up. Or maybe a miracle would happen.

But the girls couldn't wait. Some of them were already on fire as they jumped—the flames growing brighter and larger as the girls fell to their deaths. One caught the hem of her dress on a window ledge. She hung there for three minutes by her fingertips with flames nipping at her until her dress finally ripped apart and she fell to the ground.

A young man appeared at the window ledge from inside the building. He helped a series of young women to the window's ledge, pausing just long enough for a girl to jump before he hoisted the next girl up. The last girl he kissed on the lips. She jumped. And then he did too.

A United Press reporter by the name of William G. Shepard was walking through Washington Square, a block away from the building, when he spotted "a puff of smoke" coming from the factory window. He immediately ran toward the building. To his horror, he learned what he called a "new sound—a more horrible sound than description can picture." That sound was the dull report of bodies falling from eighty feet above and landing on the stone sidewalk.

Corpses piled up on the sidewalk as firemen turned their attention to putting out the flames inside the building. Bystanders alerted emergency personnel when they spotted a girl moving in the bottom of a pile of bodies. They rushed to pull her out from the dead. For two minutes, she was able to breathe clean air before she expired.

AN INEVITABLE TRAGEDY

Five hundred people came to work that Saturday. Many died inside the factory. Some died later in a hospital bed or on the sidewalk. Altogether the fire claimed 146 people. Sixteen men died—some boys, but mostly adults. It was the girls—most of whom worked on the ninth floor—who suffered the most. One hundred and thirty of the victims were women—the majority teenagers who were just beginning their new lives.

While it probably seemed like a lifetime to those people who suffered inside the building, firemen had it under control in about eighteen minutes—although it took ten more minutes to fully soak the floors involved. By 5:15, the building was silent, and all that remained were bodies. Fire Chief Edward Croker described the horrific scene as "bodies burned to bare bones" and "skeletons behind sewing machines." Firemen and policemen began the emotional task of looking for survivors.

FIREMEN SEARCHING FOR BODIES 3/26/11

Firemen search for bodies in the aftermath of the fire.

After hours of searching, they found one survivor in the water at the bottom of an elevator shaft. It must have seemed like a miracle. The next day, Croker returned and found a live mouse. In tears, he gently picked up the mouse and took it home with him. "It's alive," he said. "At least it's alive."

Lots of material factors contributed to the fire that day, including especially that lit cigarette. But the general lack of planning and absence of safety training or procedures did nothing to help the people inside, or the ultimate death toll. Hundreds of people suffered because the factory owners—and the American government itself—failed to care enough about those employees to protect them.

The Triangle owners, Max Blanck and Isaac Harris, were indicted for manslaughter on April 11, 1911. (See Chapter 4 for more information about the trial and to learn about the fates of Blanck and Harris.)

But it wasn't just individuals who were responsible for the Triangle Factory fire. The tragedy was as much a result of the time period and American cultural values as anything else. Turn-of-the-twentieth-century Americans' increasing desire for cheap clothes mass-produced in factories—along with a huge influx of immigrants in need of jobs, and a labor system designed to reward the rich and exploit the poor—created a perfect storm. With so much to gain by producing millions of consumer items as quickly as possible, factory owners exploited labor without guilt and without the intervention of the government.

The Triangle tragedy was preventable, but with American culture as it was, the fire was also, sadly, inevitable.

CHAPTER 3

THE PRICE OF FASHION

Suddenly, with a strained sound, Daisy bent her head into the shirts and began to cry stormily. "They're such beautiful shirts," she sobbed, her voice muffled in the thick folds. "It makes me sad because I've never seen such—such beautiful shirts before."
—The Great Gatsby, by F. Scott Fitzgerald

There will presently be no room in the world for things; it will be filled up with the advertisements of things.
—William Dean Howells

"And I am but a machine."
—"In the Factory," by Morris Rosenfeld

The year 1900 was an exciting one in America. Not only did it signal the beginning of the twentieth century, it also followed years of unprecedented wealth. Millions of immigrants—eager to build new lives in the land of plenty—arrived during the Gilded Age, a period that lasted from roughly 1870 to the turn of the century.

While it's tempting to say that the Triangle Factory fire was caused by a cigarette butt and the careless person who discarded it, that's not entirely accurate. The Triangle fire was the result of a confluence of events, ideas, and philosophies that grew directly from the Gilded Age.

One element was the rise of mass-produced, ready-to-wear fashion, which changed American consumer culture forever.

SHOPPING IN THE GILDED AGE

If you were a teen girl from an immigrant family in the Gilded Age, you probably would have settled into American life not by starting a new school but by getting a job, likely at a factory. Factory work was plentiful, goods were cheap, and for the first time, many families had some measure of disposable income. They could buy stuff they didn't need. And buying stuff is exactly what Americans began to do. More and more consumption of everything from housewares to clothes led to an extraordinary rise in demand.

For the first time in history, regular people (that is, people who were not quite wealthy) could have multiple pieces of clothing—clothing that was ready-to-wear. Ready-to-wear meant you could walk into a store, buy a blouse, and then wear it without alteration. Prior to 1900, clothing was often custom-made by a tailor or a seamstress, which required a serious investment of time and money. Poor people had to make their own clothes, an activity that required materials and time to devote to handiwork. The rise of ready-to-wear items—along with a rise in department stores that allowed people to look at what was on offer—changed the face of fashion. Suddenly, it was easy to buy clothes (assuming a person had a few spare dollars), and it was fun to acquire them.

READY TO BUY

Ready-to-wear wasn't always fashionable, though. For centuries, ready-to-wear clothes were associated with people who were far from fashion icons. For instance, in the 1700s, sailors would buy one outfit, called a slop, at a market and wear it for a year or so. When the sailor needed new duds, he waited until he got to land, and then he purchased another slop. Slops were loose smocks with baggy pants that fit without special tailoring. Later, during the Civil War, soldiers needed uniforms faster than tailors could custom make. Smart tailors figured out that it was quicker and easier to make uniforms in a range of sizes to hand out to soldiers as needed. Those sizes were standardized later, making it easier to find ready-to-wear uniforms that fit. Prior to the Civil War, the only other people besides sailors who had ready-made clothes were slaves, and that was largely because they weren't given the time to make their own.

Though it's hard to imagine a time when people didn't have a closet full of clothes, that was often the case prior to the rise of ready-to-wear fashion. Rich people have always had plenty of clothing, but the growth of manufacturing factories opened the door to fashion for middle-class and working-class people, too. Ready-to-wear clothing could be made to look like tailor-made clothes, albeit with cheaper materials and lower standards of workmanship. Yet the availability of inexpensive clothes meant it became harder to tell who was rich and who wasn't just by looking at their outfits.

In the late 1800s, Americans began to fill their closets and dresser drawers like never before. As a result, more and more garment factories sprouted up in major cities. New York City and Philadelphia were home to the most clothing factories. Manhattan alone had 450 textile factories, which together employed some 40,000 garment workers. By the late 1800s, 70 percent of women's clothing in the United States came from a factory in Manhattan.

If you were a woman in the 1800s, you would have worn dresses. In the late 1800s, however, factories introduced a new garment that took the world by storm. That garment was the shirtwaist, a ready-to-wear, button-down blouse. The pattern was based on men's shirts, but by 1900 manufacturers were adding all sorts of fashionable and feminine flourishes. A fancy shirtwaist might have lace, frills, pleats, or embroidered stitching on the sleeves, neck, or bodice. An elegant shirtwaist would be made of fine silk or linen. Some of the most expensive shirtwaists had buttons up the back, requiring the wearer to have help getting dressed. Not all shirtwaists were fancy. Some were manufactured using cheap cotton. That meant that even factory girls, who were poorly paid (often disgustingly so), could afford a plain white shirtwaist or two.

Early versions of the shirtwaist had a lot of pleats and puffy sleeves. By the later 1800s, the fashion moved to regularly fitted shoulders. Starting in the 1910s, many women were wearing shirtwaists untucked, which eventually ushered in the dropped-waist flapper style of the 1920s.

A shirtwaist was highly versatile because it could be worn tucked into a skirt, or it could be worn under a jacket as part of a skirt suit. Manufacturers began producing shirtwaists in a range of colors, which allowed wearers to mix and match—an easy way to multiply their wardrobe!

It's hard to express just how popular shirtwaists were at the turn of the twentieth century. But here's a comparison that might give you some idea: Having a shirtwaist then was like having a pair of jeans now. Like jeans, a shirtwaist was an item of clothing that became a staple, and every woman had at least one. Imagine if I opened your closet and told you to get rid of your jeans. Sure, you might find other things to wear for a few days, but before long you'd probably miss having your favorite denim. For most people, getting dressed without jeans would be a bit of a challenge. That's exactly how girls and women in the late 1800s and early 1900s felt about their shirtwaists. Without them, what would they wear?

SHIRTWAISTS AS A SYMBOL FOR THE MODERN WOMAN

While the shirtwaist was certainly trendy, the popularity of the garment wasn't just driven by fashion. Women, especially middle-class and working-class women, liked shirtwaists for a number of practical reasons. First, the availability of such blouses freed women from always having to wear dresses. Dresses required corsets or other uncomfortable undergarments, which hindered movement. A shirtwaist was looser, and although it certainly could be worn with a corset if a woman so chose, it didn't have to be. Women finally had another option. (And not surprisingly, corsets soon began to go out of style.)

Second, because a woman could now mix and match, she could appear to have a larger wardrobe. Two skirts and two blouses meant four outfit combinations, whereas two dresses were just, well, two dresses. And two shirtwaists were significantly cheaper than even one dress.

Third, shirtwaists were an unexpected symbol of democracy. Fashion was once the sole province of the rich, but the rise of cheap clothing meant that all women—regardless of socioeconomic status—could express themselves through clothing. Prior to mass production and department stores, a poor person either had to take time to make her own clothing, or she wore hand-me-downs from other people, typically purchased from a pushcart. Shirtwaists meant that even the poorest woman could "pass" as a lady with a clean and pressed blouse.

Finally, shirtwaists were convenient. Because they were small, they could easily be hand washed in a sink or a bowl. By owning multiple shirtwaists, a woman could forego laundry for multiple days. Freedom from laundry was a very big deal. Even in the early 1900s, a time of technological growth, laundry was still grueling labor.

For all of these reasons, the demand for shirtwaists was huge. That demand meant factories needed to pump out as many shirtwaists as they possibly could. (As you will see in Chapter 3, factories in the 1900s found ways to cut costs and increase production at the expense of human labor.) Shirtwaists introduced Americans to cheap fashion, and once they had a taste for it, they wanted more. Not surprisingly, Americans' appetite for fashion grew even bigger with the rise of advertising. Once advertising grabbed hold of the shirtwaist, Americans didn't just covet the clothes they saw their peers wearing; they coveted the clothes of the models displayed in the pages of their favorite magazines.

THE BIRTH OF ADVERTISING

With the availability of off-the-rack clothes, Americans saw an accompanying rise in stores dedicated to ladies' wear. And if you didn't live in the city, no problem. You could mail order your clothing from the Sears, Roebuck and Company catalog, or from Montgomery Ward.

No matter where a fashionable person bought her clothes, she wanted to know what was in style. The late 1800s and the early 1900s ushered in a practice so ubiquitous now that it's hard to imagine a time when it didn't exist (or at least when it was not widely used). That practice was advertising. In 1867 companies spent just $50 million on advertising. That's still a lot of money, but it's nothing compared to what companies spent on advertising in 1900, just thirty-three years later. Care to take a guess? Hold on to your socks because the number ballooned to $500 million! For the first time in history, Americans were inundated with choices. Advertising helped people see their options, but it also created brand loyalty. People began to care about what their purchased goods said about themselves.

Advertising covered every consumer product you could think of, but advertising for shirtwaists absolutely exploded. A reader would see ads for them most often in women's magazines or on the pages of newspapers. On the day after the Triangle fire, just to the right of a *New York Times* story about the fire, readers found a typical ad for women's clothing. This particular ad was for Saks & Company on Broadway and 34th Street in Manhattan. The ad copy told readers that anyone can afford nice clothes: "And it matters not whether you wish to buy an inexpensive little garment for 20.00 or so, or one that costs ten times as much." (Keep in mind that $20 was still a whole lot of money at

Images of shirtwaists from a 1911 Macy's catalog.

the time.) The ad goes on to reassure readers that nice "cream chiffon blouses with a net yoke and embroidery are regularly priced at 8.50, but on sale for 4.95." That's still about $100 in 1911, but a middle-class reader who saved her money would be excited to be able to buy something that elegant and expensive. Working-class girls would have shopped in less expensive stores or catalogs where they could find shirtwaists as cheap as twenty-five cents—or about $6 now.

MEET THE GIBSON GIRLS

One of the most important and far-reaching images of the late 1800s and early 1900s was that of the shirtwaisted Gibson Girls who would establish an image of a new all-American girl. Rich, poor, or middle eclass, any girl in America could aspire to be a Gibson Girl.

During the 1890s, a man by the name of Charles Dana Gibson drew an image of a girl who would go on to play a major role in the events that led to the tragic Triangle Shirtwaist Factory fire. Between the 1890s and 1900s, Gibson would draw additional Gibson Girls, all of whom represented the ideal woman in America at the time. Gibson Girls were considered standards for beauty, fashion, and glamor. They also represented a kind of independent spirit. A Gibson Girl didn't just sit around and do nothing. She was fit. She was educated. She was elegant. And she was talented, someone who was poised to enter public life. She didn't just stay home to cook and clean. She worked, just like her male counterparts. In short, she was the very image of the new ideal woman of the Gilded Age.

Gibson drew hundreds of Gibson Girls over the years, but they shared enough signature characteristics that readers immediately would recognize a Gibson Girl illustration in the pages of a magazine. A Gibson Girl was always white, well dressed (in a shirtwaist), impossibly thin waisted, and, perhaps most important of all, confident. A Gibson Girl would appear in an ad with her head held high and her eyes boldly focused on her future. A person in the 1890s who picked up almost any magazine would have seen a Gibson Girl and read her as a symbol of the modern times.

A typical "Gibson girl" illustration from Charles Dana Gibson, estimated to be from around the time of the fire.

One of Gibson's most famous Gibson Girl drawings appeared on the cover of *Scribner's* in June of 1895. She is riding a bicycle, wearing a long skirt gathered at her ankles, a corset (we know that because her waist is teeny-tiny), and a fitted shirtwaist tucked into her skirt. The shirtwaist is one of the fancy versions with a pleated front and huge, puffy sleeves. (It's hard to believe that such a thing was ever fashionable, but every decade has its own fashion atrocities.) She has her long hair styled in the Gibson Girl fashion: piled on top of her head in a loose bun with poofy sides. (If you love the Gibson Girl hairstyle, you can find oodles of YouTube tutorials showing how you can get the signature look. It requires teasing the front and sides—or even rolling the hair to get the nice rounded frame. You'll also need a pile of French hairpins to keep it all securely pinned.) Atop her poofy bun, she wears a jaunty hat. She's looking straight ahead with a neutral expression on her face. Her head is held high, probably because she's confident of the direction she's heading.

It might be hard to understand just how influential Gibson Girls were, but they were the supermodels of their time. And they were beloved. Not only did Gibson Girls appear in magazines, but they were also the subject of songs and operas. Their hairstyles and clothing, especially their shirtwaists, were copied by women and girls all across the United States. Gibson Girls were even featured in wallpaper design!

Part of the Gibson Girl popularity was the real women who inspired Gibson's drawings. He based his illustrations on actual girls of the time period, so when magazine readers saw the drawings, they were also seeing reflections of glamorous, real-life women. In just the way we admire the styles of models we see in magazines and on TV (American Apparel models come to mind in particular here), magazine readers of the late 1800s admired Gibson Girls and their shirtwaists.

Some of the real Gibson Girls—the women Charles Gibson used as models for his drawings—were admirable in their own right. Gibson's first model was his wife, Irene Langhorne Gibson. She was beautiful and rich, but she used her influence to encourage progressive changes in America. She was particularly interested in helping women and children.

She was certainly someone that magazine readers of the time could look up to.

Camille Clifford was another Gibson Girl model. In 1907 she won an international magazine contest for the girl who best embodied the spirit of the Gibson Girl. Clifford, a Belgian actress, had one particular qualification that made her the obvious choice: She had a ridiculously small waist and looked gorgeous in a shirtwaist. As the contest winner, she sang a song composed in honor of Gibson Girls. The lyrics included these gems:

> Wear a blank expression
> And a monumental curl
> And walk with a bend in your back
> Then they will call you a Gibson Girl.

The most famous Gibson Girl model was also the most controversial. Unlike Irene Gibson and Camille Clifford, Evelyn Nesbit was no angel. But she was considered the very first supermodel. Picture a very young Cindy Crawford in a shirtwaist and a skirt with the famous Gibson Girl loose bun. Nesbit's story is surprisingly contemporary—full of romance, intrigue, betrayal, and murder. It's no wonder she was the subject of every tabloid in the early 1900s.

THE CULT OF CELEBRITY

Nesbit got her show business start as a *Floradora* Girl. If you have no idea what that is, you probably aren't alone. In 1901, *Floradora* was the biggest musical of all time. Think *Hamilton* without the hip-hop. The *Floradora* plotline is too complicated to explain, but the plot wasn't what audiences loved anyway. What they loved was the Floradora Sextette. The sextette was the legendary chorus line made up of Floradora Girls in shirtwaists. The most popular of these girls was the teenaged Evelyn Nesbit.

Before entering show biz, Nesbit turned to modeling to support her mother and her brother after her father suddenly died. At the time, modeling was not a particularly respected career choice, but Nesbit didn't have a choice. She was legendarily beautiful and could make far more money as a model than she could working in a factory.

Sometime in the early 1900s, still in her early teens, Nesbit met the very rich and important Stanford White, a successful architect who was then in his late forties. White was what was known as a stage-door johnny, the name given to men who stood outside the stage door waiting for actresses after a Broadway performance to give them gifts. White couldn't offer marriage to Nesbit—he was already married and had children—but he offered Nesbit a chance to be his mistress.

Let's pause for a minute to let this sink in: Nesbit's age at the time is a little hard to pin down because of discrepancies in her reported birth year, but she was definitely no more than sixteen when she met White. He was at least forty-seven. He was also a famous womanizer who kept his wife and children in his Long Island home while he partied it up in his penthouse in Manhattan. White was apparently quite a looker at that time, but it's hard to think so now. He had a very bushy mustache indeed.

Nesbit's relationship with White started as a flirtation. He invited her and her mother to a few of his legendary parties to show off his apartment. At one party, a girl emerged from a giant pie. Good times, right? But in spite of White's infidelity, he was quite sweet, and Nesbit quickly came to love him. The two began a passionate affair.

Because White was already married, Nesbit could never be his wife. Instead, she married a wealthy Harvard graduate by the name of Harry Thaw. Thaw came from a family who'd made tons of money in railroads and mining. He traveled the world and claimed to have spent his Harvard years playing poker. In his later life, he also became a stage-door johnny, which is how he met his future wife, Evelyn Nesbit. Nesbit, however, kept up her relationship with her boyfriend, Stanford White. Not surprisingly, Thaw wasn't pleased when he discovered his wife's extracurricular activity.

In 1906, at Café Martin in New York City, more than thirty people looked on in horror when Thaw shot White dead. The resulting trial was the subject of relentless tabloid reports for months. No trial had ever been covered to this degree. The American public read every word, fascinated by the story of Evelyn Nesbit, the Gibson Girl, and her jealous husband.

Thaw was convicted and sent to prison. Nesbit did just fine for herself. She went on to become a silent film star and even ran her own speakeasy during the Prohibition years. She certainly wasn't known as the morally upstanding Gibson Girl, but she did represent a kind of glamour and intrigue that captivated America. And her sordid story also shows that we've always loved celebrity gossip!

Gibson Girls—whatever the stories of the real girls on whom they were modeled—came to be representations of what average American girls hoped to become. Shirtwaists were an important part of their image. It's no wonder that the demand for such garments seemed to grow every day.

MODERN MIDDLE-CLASS LADIES

Factory girls in the early 1900s were living in a changing time, and not just in terms of fashion. They had opportunities that previous generations never had. Their mothers and grandmothers—in America or in the old country—lived in a time when women were considered less rational than men and therefore required stringent rules to keep them from making bad decisions. When it came to sex, women were expected to be pure. Sex was just for having babies. They were to answer to their husbands. And their primary job was to make a clean and safe home for the children. Working-class women had the additional task of working outside the home in addition to all their chores at home.

The Industrial Revolution, however, provided opportunities for women to play new roles. Middle-class and working women married later, so they could work or go to school longer. When they did get married, they had fewer children. Some who received education were able to become nurses or teachers, professions that were formerly the province of men.

Working-class factory girls did have opportunities to move up into the middle class. If they were lucky, they could become sales clerks in a department stores or a secretaries. They would still work hard, but they would get vacation pay and pensions. Even better, they wouldn't have to do as much physical labor. Office jobs were less tiring and could be done longer because they weren't so physically draining. Even more important, young women who rose up in the factory ranks or found their way to department store clerk positions could be considered middle class, a highly coveted social position.

Keep in mind that at the time middle class didn't just refer to income. It described a set of values. Middle-class people worked hard, but they didn't work with their hands. They could interact with higher-class people without any problem. They were not pretentious or materialistic, and they were thrifty and demonstrated superior self-control. The common belief was that their impressive self-control is what propelled them to middle-class status in the first place.

Middle-class young ladies went on to marry middle-class men, typically foremen and managers. They worked in offices, not factory lines, and made much better money. Once married, these young women could quit working outside the home to be homemakers, a job that afforded much leisure time. Because people had fewer children, middle-class homemakers found child rearing easier than ever before. And with a little bit of extra money, many middle-class women could afford to hire help inside the home. (And who do you suppose they hired? That's right: women who weren't part of the middle class. The hired help were often immigrants or women of color who couldn't find jobs elsewhere.)

More disposable income meant that not only could middle-class ladies buy clothes and shoes, but they could also buy hygiene products with their pocket money. Because most housewives had enough time and money to read ladies' magazines, they were inundated with advertisements explaining why they absolutely needed products like shampoo, toothpaste, and deodorant—and as a result, most middle-class homes soon had these things. The housewife's job became one that involved a lot of shopping. And the more products they bought, the more need America had for factories—and factory workers—to produce its consumer goods.

GIRLS JUST WANT TO HAVE FUN

Because middle-class women and men had more time on their hands, they looked for more things to amuse themselves. In the late 1800s and early 1900s, the concept of leisure became important to Americans. Prior to this period, leisure was something only rich people had, while working people were expected to stay busy. But the changing times came with changing ideas, and one of those ideas was that fun was important. (Imagine that!) Now we assume that free time and vacations are good things—even necessary things. But back then, people were just wrapping their minds around this idea.

By the late 1800s, even working-class folks were allowed some latitude for fun, though they certainly didn't have as much money or free time as middle-class people did. Still, the Gilded Age ushered in an explosion of pleasure activities for all income levels. For instance, anyone could enjoy popular music. You could go to a dance hall and hear live music performed. Or you could buy sheet music and play the tunes yourself if you had a piano. Ragtime was particularly popular. You undoubtedly know the biggest ragtime tune of that era: "The Entertainer," by Scott Joplin. (If you've ever taken piano lessons, I'm willing to bet you learned how to play this song.) People with a bit of money could buy a phonograph and listen to records whenever they wanted. Imagine how exciting that must have been! To put Scott Joplin on your phonograph machine and feel like you were right there listening to him play must have felt like nirvana. Not surprisingly, because of the proliferation of phonographs, music became big business and led to the rise of mega pop stars. Before Beyoncé and Rihanna, there were Irving Berlin and Bessie Smith.

If you loved theater, the Gilded Age had plenty of that to offer, too. There were vaudevilles available for every taste. Vaudevilles were a kind of variety show that featured a range of acts, from jugglers to singers to comedians to dancing girls. One of Hollywood's biggest film stars got her start in vaudeville—Mae West. You may have heard of her, even though you probably haven't seen any of her films. She was quite scandalous back in the day, although we probably wouldn't think so now. Her film performances were criticized and sometimes censored because she acted sexy, made frequent sexual double entendres, and depicted women who seemed to enjoy sex and sexuality. In vaudeville, though, audiences were fine with entertainment that bordered on the raunchy. Mae West represented a vulgarity that people absolutely loved.

Even if you didn't speak English well, there was still a vaudeville performance for you. Neighborhood enclaves often put on their own performances. Italians, for instance, liked to stage operas reminiscent of those they attended back home. These were big productions with melodramatic themes. Yiddish people, on the other hand, often loved to produce comedies. Plays and skits frequently featured themes that resonated with immigrant audiences. One popular play, *Anna the Finisher*, was about a girl who sewed buttons and did embroidery work in a garment factory.

Along with vaudevilles, New York was home then—just as it is now—to some of the finest theater performances in the world. One of the most famous actors of the time was Jacob Adler, a Yiddish-speaking immigrant who performed everything from Shakespeare to Russian plays.

Movies came into existence in 1894, when Thomas Edison's kinetoscope parlor opened in New York City. People stood in line to watch a short film through a peephole. (Only one person could watch at a time, so everyone had to wait in line until it was their turn.) Not much later, the first actual movie theater opened in Buffalo, New York. In 1905, the first nickelodeon (a movie theater where admission cost just five cents) opened in Pittsburgh. It was so popular that by 1908 there were eight thousand of these theaters in the United States. Movies became so popular that by 1910 almost thirty million Americans per week visited a movie theater. And just like today, before or after taking in the cinema, people often met up with friends at clubs or restaurants, where they could talk about famous actors and dissect plotlines. Movies had the serendipitous by-product of helping immigrants improve their English. Viewers weren't just passing the time; they were learning to better navigate life in America.

For sports aficionados, the Gilded Age offered a range of spectator sports. People attended baseball games at newly built stadiums. They went to college football games and rooted for the home team, even if they'd never set foot in a college classroom. In any area of any city, you could find boxing matches, track and field games, and even bike racing. If you looked a bit farther, you'd find horse racing. And at any of these events, you could engage in gambling, which became big business.

If you were a reader, you could find plenty of reading material in many different languages. Books were fairly cheap and widely available. They offered a low-cost way to understand what life was like for all sorts of people. Reading was (and still is) a way for people to expand their worldviews and develop empathy.

Popular books included Theodore Dreiser's *Sister Carrie*, Upton Sinclair's *The Jungle*, Kate Chopin's *The Awakening*, and Stephen Crane's *Maggie: A Girl of the Streets*. All treated themes and issues that were very much on people's minds. *Sister Carrie* is about a girl who makes her way to the city only to end up a mistress and then a movie actress (neither of which were very respectable stations in life). *The Jungle* is about the horrible conditions for immigrants working in slaughterhouses. It's a critique on American capitalism as much as anything else. *The Awakening* is about a middle-class wife and mother who feels trapped by her role in the family and in society. Her ending isn't happy.

All of this must have been thrilling for people who lived in this period. We're accustomed to having a hundred different ways to amuse ourselves at any given time. But it's important to remember that the explosion of entertainment options in the Gilded Age represented a completely different philosophy of living for many people. Life didn't have to be an endless slog through work and family obligations. Life could be fun and exciting and interesting, even for those working-class people who had to labor in factories for six days a week.

Though life was far from perfect or fair in America, people from all over the world were desperate to become American citizens for the freedom, opportunity, and liberty the country offered (in spirit, if not always in practice). A tide of new immigrants from southern and eastern Europe gave their blood, sweat, and tears, and sometimes their lives, for America's manufacturing empire.

CHAPTER 4

COMING TO AMERICA

I had always hoped that this land might become a safe and agreeable asylum to the virtuous and persecuted part of mankind, to whatever nation they might belong.

—George Washington

"Give me your tired, your poor, / Your huddled masses yearning to breathe free, / The wretched refuse of your teeming shore. / Send these, the homeless, tempest-tost to me, / I lift my lamp beside the golden door."

—"The New Colossus," by Emma Lazarus

In 1892 a man by the name of Francis Bellamy penned a short verse that you might know. (In fact, you probably know it by heart.) That little verse was what Americans now know as "The Pledge of Allegiance." It was written for and delivered at the 1892 Columbus Day celebration, a massive fete that celebrated Columbus's arrival. We now recognize that Columbus is not the hero we imagined. Like other European explorers of his time, he was racist and ruthless in his treatment of Native Americans and anyone else nonwhite. But at the time, Columbus was a celebrated man, and Bellamy's "Pledge of Allegiance" created solidarity among Americans. It suggested that (in theory, anyway) all Americans were equal citizens, regardless of birth or circumstances. In practice, however, immigrants were often treated like second-class citizens, as we'll soon see.

UNPRECEDENTED IMMIGRATION IN THE UNITED STATES

Native-born Americans feared the arrival of immigrants, particularly those with notably different languages, cultures, customs, and ideologies. Fear ran deep that immigrants were socialists (people who advocated against capitalism) or anarchists (people who advocated the abolishment of all government). In truth, most immigrants wanted the same things native-born citizens wanted: the right to live a safe and happy life. They wanted to work and earn money to support their families, just like everybody else.

The same year Bellamy debuted "The Pledge of Allegiance," Ellis Island opened and began processing immigrants. From 1892 to 1924, Ellis Island welcomed twelve million people. On busy days, the facility could process thousands of people. The vetting process, though, was anything but easy. Inspectors asked every person twenty-nine questions, including why they were coming to America and what they intended to do to support themselves and their family.

In the Registry Room, doctors carefully inspected each individual for signs of disease or illness. These medical inquiries came to be known as "six-second physicals." Six seconds was the amount of time doctors had to spot a serious illness or signs of a disease.

The administration process at Ellis Island took about four hours total. That might not seem terribly long to you, but imagine how it must have felt after having spent weeks on a boat, often without proper food, toilet facilities, baths, or comfortable sleeping quarters. To add insult to injury, first- and second-class passengers were able to bypass the inspection process altogether. Officials believed that if you had enough money to purchase a first-class ticket, you probably didn't have a serious illness; nor would you be a burden to the country. So unless you had some obvious affliction, wealthier passengers would have been able to exit the ship and begin their new lives immediately.

People who traveled via steerage, however, were automatically assumed to be potential risks. For these people, there was no avoiding the lengthy inspection process. Unfortunately, even if they began the journey healthy, they may very well have acquired an illness aboard ship. Steerage was crowded and unsanitary. Passengers slept on straw mattresses tiered in multiple rows—like bunk beds. As many as four hundred people had to share two toilets, and there were no baths at all. Those unfortunate souls who were subject to seasickness often spent two weeks or more confined to their bunks, throwing up as the ship rocked on the ocean waves. It didn't take long before the entire airless lower deck was smelly and germ filled.

Even if steerage passengers survived the journey without falling ill, they still had to prove that they would be able to work and support themselves while in America—a difficult task if they didn't know English.

If they didn't pass the inspection process, they could be turned away. Remember that a doctor could say no to someone after just six seconds! Those unlucky people were then required to sail back home at their own expense, even if the rest of the family was allowed to stay. No wonder passengers nicknamed Ellis Island the "Island of Fears."

If the passengers were lucky enough to pass the test, they then got to board a ferry and travel the short distance to Manhattan, though you can imagine that getting on a boat was the very last thing they wanted to do.

Some immigrants came to America without family or friends, but many wrote letters to family members or friends who came before them. This way they could be prepared for the questions at Ellis Island, and they could line up a place to stay. They also tried to secure jobs before they arrived, and between 1880 and the mid-1920s jobs were quite plentiful.

It is perhaps hard to say definitively whether the Industrial Revolution was fueled by the arrival of immigrants or whether the expansion of industry enticed immigrants. I suspect the answer is both. Historians have shown that when the supply of jobs diminished, fewer immigrants came to America. At the same time, many immigrants came to America because the alternative was to stay in a country where they might starve or be killed by their own government (more on that in a bit). Regardless of why immigrants came, they provided an unprecedented number of workers for America's booming factories, including the garment factories.

TWENTY MILLION IMMIGRANTS

As the factories grew, more workers were needed. Between 1815 and 1880, more than eight million immigrants came to America, helping to fuel the rise of industry and a movement in American history called the new immigration. Between 1880 and 1924, more than twenty million immigrants arrived. Let's try to put that in perspective: twenty million is equivalent to the 2015 population of New York City, Los Angeles, Chicago, Houston, Philadelphia, and Phoenix put together!

No other nation accepted more immigrants than the United States. For those immigrants searching for economic freedom and opportunity, America must have seemed like a paradise, a heaven on earth. That's not to say that America was a heaven on earth, as we will see, but the country did provide asylum to people who were all but forced to leave their homes across the ocean.

THE GIRLS FROM EASTERN EUROPE

Let's go back to the factory girls we met in the first chapter. Two, Bessie Gabrilowich and Fannie Lansner, were born in Russia and immigrated to the United States at a fairly young age. Though it's difficult to track down information about their specific families and their individual situations prior to their arrival in America, we do know a lot about Russian immigration at the time. That information gives us a window into what it would have been like for other eastern European immigrants.

Like Bessie and Fannie, most eastern European immigrants were Jewish. During the late 1800s and early 1900s, fully one third of the world's Jewish people emigrated to America. Two million Jews came to America between 1881 and 1914, the beginning of World War I. Prior to 1880, most Americans were of British, German, or Irish de-

Eastern European immigrants aboard the S.S. Amsterdam.

scent. After 1880, America became more diverse in large part because of the Jewish population. That number isn't surprising when you look at what was happening to Jewish people in Russia.

Political strife in Russia began in the late 1700s when the country seized a part of Poland, the very place where most Jews lived. (After World War I, Poland would regain its independence, but until 1918 it would remain under Russian control.)

Discrimination against Jewish people persevered for hundreds of years. By 1900 that discrimination had reached full-on hatred. Russian czars separated Jewish people from other people by forcing Jews into what was called the Pale of Settlement. Pale means "fence," but in this case, there was no real fence, just a line on a map that separated Jewish settlements from others. In general, Jews were not allowed "beyond the Pale," unless they were skilled artisans or merchants. By 1900 almost five million Jews were living within the Pale in shtetls, or small towns, where little opportunity existed.

The Russian state treated families like Bessie's and Fannie's horribly. The level of persecution may be hard to imagine now, but the Russian government dreamed up so many laws designed to limit Jewish people's rights that the laws filled a thousand-page book. Not only did the Russian government discriminate—by limiting job opportunities and forcing Jewish families into the Pale—but it also sanctioned violence.

Like many other Jewish families in Russia, Bessie's and Fannie's families were constantly under threat of something called a pogrom. A pogrom was basically a legal riot against Jewish people. Whenever something bad happened—something was stolen, or someone was hurt—Jewish people were blamed, even if they had absolutely no responsibility for what occurred. Thousands of Jewish people were killed in pogroms in the early 1900s. For many Jews, leaving Russia wasn't just an opportunity to have a better life. It was, in very many cases, the only way to save their lives.

Eastern Europeans who didn't face persecution at home still had reason to leave their countries. That's because some countries required military conscription, meaning that the government could compel you to join the military for some specified period of time. Some countries required service for up to twenty-five years!

If military conscription didn't turn people away, overcrowding might have contributed to a person's decision to emigrate. Eastern Europe saw a 75 percent increase in population between 1860 and 1910. More people meant less space, and before long there simply wasn't enough farmland or jobs available. Europe was highly industrialized in major cities, where many eastern Europeans could have found factory jobs. The problem was that many skilled workers were put out of business because of the factories. A successful cobbler, for instance, might have spent years developing his craft and building experience as an artisan and small-business owner. When factories opened, that cobbler would have had to close his shop since the factories could produce more shoes for less money. Many of these skilled laborers simply couldn't support their families while working at a low-paying factory job, so some decided to try their luck in America instead. (Some of these same people ended up doing low-paid factory work in the United States anyway.)

Settling in New York City made sense for many immigrants. New York offered jobs—millions of them. It was a city that was hospitable to immigrants, so the population grew. In 1911, the same year as the Triangle fire, 75 percent of New Yorkers were immigrants or children of immigrants.

But it wasn't easy being an immigrant. Of the fifteen million immigrants who came to America between 1900 and 1910, most were from non-English-speaking nations. They often found it hard to adjust to the crowded cities where they were expected to do jobs that native-born citizens refused to do.

THE GIRLS FROM ITALY

Things weren't much better in Italy, where Kate Leone's family came from. Recall that Kate was just fourteen years old at the time of the fire. She was younger than the others and found herself in a pack of girls fighting to get to the elevator. Like many of her coworkers at the factory, she was born in the United States. Her parents emigrated from Germany, but her father's name—Leone—suggests that he originally came from Italy. He would certainly have good reason to leave Italy at the time.

In the late 1800s, Italy was almost like two different countries. Northern Italy was tourist country and was economically developed, but Southern Italy was rural. People made their living in the south as farmers or by working in small villages, and they were required to pay a ton of taxes to the north. On top of that, Southern Italians also faced a lot of prejudice in their own country. They were frequently referred to as "Black Italians," a name meant to disparage them and suggest a lesser status.

For those Southern Italians who managed to get by, in spite of all the strikes against them, they would still face great hardship in the 1880s and early 1900s. Heavy rainfall led to the formation of swamps in Southern Italy, breeding large mosquito outbreaks. This contributed to an outbreak of malaria that claimed many lives. Southern Italians were then later devastated by the 1905 Calabria earthquake, a natural disaster that killed hundreds of people. Just one year later Vesuvius erupted and killed hundreds more people in the Naples area. More than 150,000 people fled the ravaged land. To make matters worse, in 1908 a tsunami struck the Strait of Messina, with waves reaching forty miles inland. (To put that in perspective, Maui is forty-eight miles long. The Strait of Messina tsunami would have covered the entire island of Maui!) Tragically, 100,000 people died in that tsunami.

All that devastation in Italy must have made people feel like they were doomed. Understandably, Southern Italians fled their country looking for new lives. Between 1880—the start of the malaria outbreaks—and 1921, four million Italians immigrated to the United States, hoping to avoid the devastation that had been wrought on their beloved home. Some joined family members who were already in America. Others used the services of padrones, a type of agent who offered Italians labor contracts. Such contracts sometimes amounted to nothing more than legalized slavery.

A ticket from Italy to America was around $34, which was still a lot of money, equivalent to about $1,000 now. But it was the kind of money that a motivated person could save up if he was hardworking and thrifty. Things in Italy had gotten so bad that many people felt they had no choice but to leave.

THE GIRLS FROM AUSTRIA-HUNGARY

Another major source of immigrants was Austria-Hungary. Two factory girls we met in Chapter 1 had ties to the unified empire. Annie Miller, the courageous girl who ran back inside the factory to help her friends, was born in America, but her parents emigrated from Austria-Hungary. Rose Rosenfeld, who ran up to the tenth floor to see how the executives were escaping the fire, came to America from Austria-Hungary as a very young girl with her parents. As with the other girls we've met, we don't know much about why these particular families immigrated to America, but we do know a lot about why Austrians left their homeland. They faced many of the same hardships and prejudices as the Italians and Russians.

Austria-Hungary was a massive empire consisting of multiple current nations including Austria, Hungary, Serbia, Slovenia, and the Czech Republic. In the early days of the empire—the 1700s—Austria-Hungary was usually referred to as the Habsburg Empire. So when people came to America and listed Austria as their nationality, they might have been from any number of eastern European groups. In the 1800s, though, people started to identify more strongly with their individual linguistic and social cultures. For that reason, even though a German-Austrian and a Hungarian-Austrian may have hailed from the same country, they would have had very different beliefs and practices. In America, they might not identify with each other at all, though native-born Americans probably would have lumped them together in one category.

Regardless of where in the empire Austro-Hungarians hailed, they came to America for good reasons. Four million people set sail from Austrian ports and arrived on American soil between 1880 and 1919. They left their homes for different reasons, but three main factors pushed Austro-Hungarians to America. First, in 1848 Austro-Hungarian peasants were emancipated. That meant they finally had the freedom to leave home and find better jobs to support their families. Second, while some newly freed peasants found jobs at home, many discovered there simply wasn't enough work to go around. That's because the population of the empire had dramatically increased. More people meant more competition for land and for jobs on farms. Finally, changes in the political and economic spheres led to an increase in nationalism. Austro-Hungarians, particularly those who didn't have a lot of money, status, or power, worried that their rights would be curtailed. Thus, immigrants fled to America hoping for equality and acceptance.

RACISM AND XENOPHOBIA IN AMERICA

Slavs—people from specific areas of southern and eastern Europe, like Bessie and Fannie and their families—suffered particularly egregious forms of discrimination. Americans in the early 1900s frequently looked down on immigrant Slavs for no other reasons than racism. Northern and western Europeans—from places like Great Britain, Ireland, and Germany—considered themselves superior people who were better equipped to assimilate into American life. Of course, that's not true at all, but racism is never logical. It comes from a place of fear and hate for people who look different, behave differently, and believe different things. That fear of difference is called xenophobia.

Slavs were different from native-born Americans in a couple of important ways. First, most Slavic immigrants were Jewish or Catholic, which alarmed many American-born Protestants. Second, white native-born Americans often preferred immigrants with formal education and high skills. Many eastern and southern Europeans left home precisely because they needed education and marketable skills, and they came to America hoping to find those very things. When they arrived, they may have found work in factories, but they didn't always find access to education or job training. Without skills, including language skills, new immigrants had little chance of finding jobs that would allow them to rise above their poverty.

One of the most insidious effects of racism is the way it dehumanizes its targets. The pervasive (and very wrong-headed) belief that certain immigrants were somehow fundamentally different from others—and from white American-born Protestants—made it easier for people to ignore the plight of new immigrants. Let's put it this way: If you believe that another person is somehow less of a human than you are, you'll find it easier to treat them worse. And you may even start to believe that your neighbor's unfortunate conditions are his or her own fault.

It should be said, of course, that immigrants were not the only people in America in the 1900s who suffered from profound forms of discrimination. Eastern and southern European immigrants, for all the hurdles they faced, still looked a lot like the American citizens (former European immigrants themselves) who now sought to keep them out. Gilded Age America's treatment of nonwhite immigrants—and of its own Native American and African American population—was predictably deplorable. African Americans and Native Americans were not able, for the most part, to find work in urban factories.

So bear in mind that while new immigrants faced rampant racism, they weren't the only groups who experienced such regrettable treatment.

LIFE FOR IMMIGRANTS IN NEW YORK CITY

Many immigrants came to America believing that they were moving to a virtual paradise. That isn't what they found. Life for an immigrant in the early 1900s was about as difficult as you can imagine. One Italian immigrant summed it up nicely: "I came to America because I heard the streets were paved with gold. When I got here, I found out three things: First, the streets weren't paved with gold; second, they weren't paved at all; and third, I was expected to pave them."

Life in the city was a constant struggle. For one thing, it was crowded. By 1890, one in three Americans was a city dweller. Look at it this way: In 1860 only nine American cities had more than 100,000 residents. By 1900, America boasted thirty-eight cities with more than 100,000 people. That's more than four times as many cities in just forty years. And urban areas grew like crazy. By 1920, more than half of all Americans lived in a city. The rise of industrialized agriculture meant that it was finally possible for urban dwellers to have food without growing it themselves.

With all those people crowded into such small geographic areas, cities got really dirty really fast. And it wasn't just the people who made them dirty; it was the animals as well. Manhattan was full of horses, largely because they provided an excellent mode of transportation. In the early 1900s, New York City was home to about 12,500 horses. And all those horses also produced a whole lot of poop. Manhattan streets were filled with poop. Manure piles sometimes grew as high as twenty-five feet. (If you cloned NBA player Lebron James and stood two clones atop the shoulders of the original Lebron, you would still need five more inches to get twenty-five feet!) Big poop piles aren't surprising when you consider that Manhattan's thousands of horses produced about 133 tons of poop per day. That's a little more than half the weight of the Statute of Liberty!

All that manure made for a dangerous environment. When it rained, the poop turned into manure swamps. When it didn't rain, the swamps dried up and the poop turned to dust. That dust would blow everywhere, including into people's eyes and mouths. Every year people died from manure dust. While death is rarely welcome, I would imagine dying by poop dust ranks near the top of embarrassing ways to go.

You'd think that the New Yorkers would have gotten to work cleaning up the streets, but, well, the street cleaners were part of the problem. Like many other city workers, street cleaners made backroom contracts with government officials who were buying votes or offering kickbacks. All that wheeling and dealing meant that street cleaners were often locked in negotiations or, alternatively, had won contracts for jobs they couldn't actually do. Things did get better in 1904, though, when subways opened limited lines. And as more people got cars, fewer horses were left to poop in the street. (Of course, cars emit their own kind of dangerous pollution.)

The inside of apartment buildings wasn't much better than the streets. As immigrants flooded into New York City, landlords rushed to rent whatever they could. They converted single-family homes into multifamily spaces; they rented dank basements and smelly stables; they even rented space in warehouses and defunct factories. In some blocks of New York City, eight hundred people crowded into an acre of space. Here's a handy way to envision that many people in one space: Imagine the basketball court in your school gym. Now imagine that you put twelve of them side by side. That's a little more than an acre. Now let's say that your school's basketball team has fifteen members. Invite fifty-two other teams to your school to live in your twelve basketball courts. That's a lot of people in a small area, especially when you imagine that your basketball courts need to include streets, apartment buildings, and shops. And horse poo.

Because so many people needed homes, tenement buildings (the word "tenement" usually implies low-rent, low-quality housing for poorer renters in urban areas) began popping up all over New York City. In 1900, 1.6 million New Yorkers lived in tenements. By 1909, New York City was home to 100,000 tenement buildings.

Tenements were hardly fancy or comfortable. They usually had just two rooms—a parlor and a bedroom. Bathrooms were a luxury; instead, privies (which we might call outhouses) and water pumps were shared by multiple families. Those privies were prone to overflowing into the street, adding to the giant piles of waste.

Entire families would crowd into these two-room spaces, and if they had any room left, they would rent floor space to those who weren't able to afford their own apartments. A lucky immigrant in the early 1900s with a bit more money in his pocket could find a three-room apartment for about $8 a month, which would be less than $200 now.

Regardless of size or price, apartments were almost always full. Kids slept three or four to a bed. Boarders slept wherever they could and bathed in sinks. Living in a tenement all but guaranteed that you'd never have any kind of privacy, but people made it work because they had no other choice.

Part of the problem with tenements in general was the way they were constructed in the first place. Sometimes called dumbbell tenements (named after their shape), these apartments were built so they could fit side by side on each end of the "dumbbell," with bathroom facilities in the middle. (In 1901 the United States government passed a law requiring all tenements to have running water, bathrooms, and at least one window.) The space on the "dumbbell" ends was then divided into two separate apartments. That meant only one room in an apartment would get any light from a window.

The one window in an apartment did provide the opportunity

for tenants to hang clotheslines, strung from one building to another, in order to dry their laundry. Clotheslines were certainly a free way to get dry laundry, but open windows caused other problems. Remember all that horse poop outside? Those piles provided prime breeding space for big, fat flies. During the hottest days of summer, people left their windows and doors open as much as they could in the hopes of getting even a small breeze to cool themselves. The flies welcomed themselves everywhere they could find food. And with the doors and windows open, tenants were subject to the constant noise outside. From the sounds of the elevated trains to the peddlers hollering at potential buyers, New York City was never quiet. On top of that, open doors and windows meant that grime and dirt—from all the construction outside—covered every surface, from inside apartments to the clothes people wore outside and to work. Factories were pretty dirty places anyway, so hardly anybody ever felt clean.

Because of all that grime, laundry was a big deal. Everything was dirty, but you couldn't just put clothes in a washing machine and have them emerge clean like magic. Laundry was backbreaking labor. Women filled laundry tubs with gas-heated hot water. They then scrubbed the clothes over washboards. From there, they had to starch the garments and wring them dry. They heated irons over coal stoves to press the materials. And then of course it didn't take long before the clothes were filthy again, which meant the washing process had to start anew.

Tenement life and everything that accompanied it—from sharing a bathroom to washing clothes—was hard. Undoubtedly, immigrants worked hard just to keep themselves and their families fed, clothed, and housed. It must have seemed like the deck was stacked against them from the start. If they got sick, they couldn't work. If they were injured on the job, they couldn't work, and there was no workers' compensation, unemployment wages, health insurance, or Medicare. Those who were sick simply couldn't work. And if they couldn't work, the landlord would evict them by placing their belongings outside, where items could easily be stolen or destroyed. If they died at work, they left their family behind, now short one income. And death at work was a real threat. In 1911 alone, 50,000 Americans died on the job.

Once at work, even a perfectly healthy person might lose his or her job. Factories were constantly finding ways to cut costs, firing those who earned higher wages to replace them with people who would accept less.

We now live in a time when governmental safety nets exist for those who cannot work. (It's not a perfect system, mind you. Many people in America still worry about their livelihoods in an uncertain economy.) Employment concerns today are generally left to adults. But back then, teens also had to worry about work; their families depended on them. Kate, Annie, Rose, and Bessie all contributed to their family's living expenses. Without their paychecks, they wouldn't

The girl on the right was an estimated fourteen years old when this picture was taken, in 1908, at a sweatshop on Ridge Street.

be able to pay the rent or buy food. Fannie, just a few years older than the others, had no family in the United States, so her job was the sole means of supporting herself. Plus, like many others, she had to save money to bring her family to the United States. She was probably sending money to them as well.

If you're a teenager in America in the twenty-first century, your job is likely quite simple: You go to school. The law requires you to stay in school until you are at least sixteen. In the early 1900s, school was a luxury that few immigrants could afford, and college was a faraway and largely unattainable dream. A lifetime of hard work was the fate for most people. You probably have hopes of a future career, which almost certainly isn't working in a factory for twelve hours a day. Nor does it involve having lots of children go to work as soon as they are old enough to thread a needle or operate a simple machine. What would it be like to know that you would spend your life in a factory with no other prospects? It was a pretty grim time for most immigrants.

CHAPTER 5

THE SELF-MADE MAN

We have always known that heedless self-interest was bad morals; we now know that it is bad economics.
—Franklin Delano Roosevelt

"It reminds me of Cinderella," said Dick, "when she was changed into a fairy princess. I see it one night at Barnum's. What'll Johnny Nolan say when he sees me? He won't dare to speak to such a young swell as I be now. Ain't it rich?" and Dick burst into a loud laugh.
—*Ragged Dick,* by Horatio Alger

We all hope to find a career that's financially viable and emotionally satisfying. We want to be passionate about our work. We want to be interested and invested in our jobs. The luckiest among us will have access to education and training that will allow us to fulfill these goals. In the late 1800s and early 1900s, though, work was a means of survival, even while the deck was stacked against the workers. That's because the economic system was set up to exploit workers while maximizing the profits of the owners.

ECONOMIC INDIVIDUALISM

During the Gilded Age (and after), many Americans believed that poverty was a moral failing. The prevailing belief was that working-class people—people like Kate, Annie, Rose, Bessie, and Fannie—just needed to demonstrate more self-control. The idea was that poor people wouldn't be poor if they just worked harder and quit squandering opportunities. With the young girls in the Triangle Factory in mind, however, we know that American immigrants worked very hard, so it's pretty insulting to suggest that their poverty was their fault. The truth was that poverty was a result of a system that was rigged to take advantage of people's labor while lining the pockets of those who controlled production (and that's still true to a large extent today).

Something else happened that made life even more difficult for working-class Americans. In the early 1900s, America witnessed the rise of corporations—companies made up of many people or shareholders who acted as one entity. In 1904 three hundred corporations controlled about 40 percent of all manufacturing. That's a lot already. But by 1929, two hundred corporations owned almost 50 percent of all manufacturing and almost 60 percent of all capital assets (land, buildings, etc.). The rise of corporations in the Gilded Age represented a new age of "economic individualism," where people pursued wealth at the expense of everyone else. Prior to this idea of every man for himself, Americans assumed that businesses existed for the good of everyone. The new corporations—impersonal and disconnected from labor sources—were simply vehicles for a few people to make obscene amounts of money.

That corporate system influenced everything in America, from culture to values to how people lived their lives in general. During the Gilded Age, Americans were inundated with images of the self-made man, the ideal that everyone was supposed to aspire to. The self-made person was generally conceived of as someone who came from modest roots and worked his way to the top through hard work, tenacity, and dedication. This image was so popular that a man by the name of Horatio Alger wrote a whole series of books about self-made men. His most famous character was Ragged Dick. Raggedy Dick, in Alger's novels, is a boy from the streets who starts out as a shoeshine boy but who works his way out and becomes quite wealthy and respectable. Wealthy people in the Gilded Age loved to trot out Ragged Dick as an example to which all immigrants should aspire. Many of those wealthy people told their own "Ragged Dick" stories about themselves as a way to feel superior about their wealth and social position. They desperately believed that they were rich because they deserved it, which meant they didn't have to feel guilty about poor people. If you were poor, you deserved it, so the thinking went.

The Ragged Dick story, however, is just a story. For one thing, Dick doesn't become wealthy through hard work alone. He gets really lucky. If you look at the story closely, you'll see that Dick is fortunate enough to shine the shoes of an important man who invites him to church and introduces him to other important people. Dick is lucky to have a roommate who teaches him how to read and write. He is in the right place at the right time when he rescues a drowning child, and the child's wealthy father gives him a nice suit and a job. Certainly, Dick demonstrates hard work, cleverness, and frugality, but more importantly, he is one lucky kid. All that luck suggests that the writer, Horatio Alger, might have understood that the self-made man didn't necessarily exist.

Outside of stories, the self-made man was indeed a fantasy. Even the men in real life who claimed to be self-made often were not. Most of the wealthiest men in America at the time—and there were some extremely wealthy people—were not uneducated immigrants who started with nothing. They were men who had some education, family support, and incredible opportunities that others didn't have. Ragged Dick only seems true because it's our greatest wish—that a poor person can become rich simply by his or her own hard work and wits. We've actually convinced ourselves it is true. That's the unfortunate legacy of the Gilded Age.

Gilded Age ideas about poverty in America can be summed up by a guy named George E. Waring. In 1878 he spoke on the occasion of a contest (sponsored by an organization with the unenticing name of The Plumber and the Sanitation Engineer) to find the best design for housing "working people." Waring gave a speech prior to handing out the award to the contest winner and said: "As a rule they [poor people] will live like pigs, and die like sheep, unless they are compelled to live decently and prevented by the strong protection of authority against evils over which they have no control."

That's pretty awful, right? But that's how people thought of the poor at the time. (One could argue that some people still think about poverty this way.)

Are you curious about which design won the contest? It was James Ware, the person who designed dumbbell tenements, those cramped, windowless apartments that made millions of people miserable for years.

THE FIRST MILLIONAIRES IN AMERICA

Men with exceptional opportunity were few and far between. But those who were rich were stinking rich. John Jacob Astor, founder of the Astor House, the legendary New York City hotel, is now considered the first millionaire in America. When he died in 1848 at the age of eighty-four, he was worth between $20 and $30 million. That doesn't seem like all that much now (although I'd certainly take $20 million if you offered it to me), but it was an unheard of amount of money in the mid-1880s.

Opened in May of 1836, the Astor House was a half-million-dollar property designed to be the talk of the city. Prior to the Astor House (and the fancy Tremont House in Boston, the first modern hotel in America), hotels in America really didn't exist. People stayed in small taverns or inns. The Astor House was so luxurious that people came there just for the fun of it, a notion completely unheard of in New York City before then. Of course, you had to be very rich to afford a night there.

By the 1880s, Astor-level wealth was much more common. Just thirty-some years after Astor's death, America was home to many millionaires. And a lot of the wealthy lived on Fifth Avenue in Manhattan, a neighborhood that came to be known as Millionaires' Row. Along with Astor's descendants, the block included such fabulously wealthy families as the Morgans (of the banking empire) and the Vanderbilts (of the railroad and shipping empire).

The Manhattan millionaires didn't limit themselves to real estate in the city. They all had summerhouses in various glamorous locations. (Only the poor and undistinguished middle classes spent summers in the hot and humid city.) The Vanderbilts summered on Newport, Rhode Island, at their home called The Breakers. The summerhouse mansion was 140,000 square feet. (Just to put that size in perspective, in 2014 the median size of an American home was 2,453 square feet. That means that fifty-seven median-sized American homes could fit into the Vanderbilts' summer home!) The house had thirty-seven rooms for the family and thirty-three rooms for servants. After the house was built in 1883, for the hefty price of $7 million (that's closer to $48 million now), Mrs. Vanderbilt had a $250,000 housewarming costume ball and invited a thousand of her closest friends as guests. Her attendees came dressed as European aristocrats, like Louis XIV and Marie Antoinette. The Vanderbilts only used the house for a few weeks in July and August (and maybe for a party or two in the winter). For the most part, their summer home sat unused while they rotated among all their other properties.

Mrs. Vanderbilt wasn't the only party animal of the time. The Gilded Age rich were known for their extravagant fetes where they conspicuously showed just how wealthy they were. Take Caroline Webster Schermerhorn. She married William Astor, son of John Jacob Astor. Caroline Astor loved big parties, in part because they allowed her and William to display their wealth. She particularly loved having midnight suppers at their Fifth Avenue mansion. Guests would be served fish, beef, duck, partridge, quail, and foie gras on gold and silver dishes. And that was just the main course.

The Astors had eighteen live-in staff members to help with these parties, plus outside caterers for the food and flowers. Staff could be as many as 125 for any given party. They wore uniforms that were finer than a factory worker's Sunday best: green coats with white short pants, black stockings, and red vests with gold buttons.

Caroline Astor wore a fancy wig to cover her gray hair. She loved the color purple and insisted upon velvet, silk, or satin materials. She wasn't afraid to show off her jewelry either. At her last party in 1905, she wore a tiara, a pearl necklace with diamond pendants, a diamond corsage, and multiple diamond and pearl pins.

Caroline Astor's peers spent ridiculous amounts of money on similar displays. Someone by the name of CKG Billings of Chicago once had a dinner served on horseback. An unnamed millionaire replaced his teeth with diamonds, for lack of better ideas about how to spend his money. Mrs. Stuyvesant Fish threw a birthday party for her dog and gifted it a $15,000 diamond collar; she also allegedly threw a dinner in honor of a monkey who wore a suit to the festivities.

Not surprisingly, regular people—people who weren't filthy rich—mocked these outlandish displays. Frederick Townsend Martin even wrote a book about how the rich lived, called *The Passing of the Idle Rich*, published in 1911. Martin wisely notes the problem with an endless supply of unthinkable sums of money:

> "There is a vast difference between the healthy, wholesome spending of money for amusements, pleasures and recreations and the feverish searching for some new sensation that can be had only at a tremendous cost. The simple expenditure of money, even in startling amounts, eventually fails to produce the thrill it ought to have [...]."

An entire medical diagnosis emerged to explain the mental state of the super rich. George M. Beard called it neurasthenia. His widely read treatise on the subject, *American Nervousness*, was published in 1884 and compared the human nervous system to a machine. When faced with too many pressures of modern life, the machine fails to function properly. Anybody could suffer neurasthenia, whether rich or poor. Still, I think we can all agree that it's easier to feel sorry for the poor person stuck in a factory than the rich person who spends his or her money on a monkey tuxedo and then feels empty.

THE GILDED AGE LEGACY

After reading about these fabulously rich people, you might think the Gilded Age was pretty great if you were rich and powerful. That's probably true. And all that wealth did contribute to a booming economy. All those factories owned by rich people did create jobs, and jobs gave immigrants opportunities—which many of them didn't have before they came to America. The availability of jobs meant higher wages for some people as well. With more money came more education, better nutrition, and better all-around living. For those reasons, life expectancy increased. Workers who were lucky made better lives for their families and lived happier existences.

But the Gilded Age's emphasis on accruing massive amounts of wealth at all costs—for just a handful of people—shaped American life for years and years to come. Pervasive political apathy toward the plight of the worker, along with economic, labor, and social policies that favored owners and managers rather than workers, led to an inevitable outcome: massive class divisions.

The people with all the money came to believe that wealth was their God-given right. They also came to believe that poor people deserved their paltry wages and horrid working conditions. The middle class was grateful to be making wages that provided a relatively easy living. Plus, they dreamed of one day moving up and into the world of the upper crust, never mind that such economic and social mobility rarely happened. Carl Degler, eminent historian, stated it best: "The men who were getting to the top, even in the 1870s—that alleged era of the self-made man—had not been poor farm boys or uneducated immigrant lads starting at the bottom, but instead men who had been given rather exceptional opportunities to make the race to the top."

The Gilded Age drew to a close around 1900, leaving a tragic legacy for workers. All those girls in the Triangle Shirtwaist Factory in 1911 were victims of an era that bred greed through unrestrained capitalism. With no motivation to protect workers—and a belief that more workers would always be available to work repetitive and unsafe jobs—factory owners and politicians alike lacked any incentive to change the system. Something had to happen to signal the alarm. Some people had to die in order for the system to change.

CHAPTER 6
LIFE IN THE FACTORY

In an assembly line, the smaller the piece of work assigned to any single individual, the less skill it requires, and the less likely the possibility that doing it well will lead to doing something more interesting and better paid.

—Jill Lepore

"Our lives shall not be sweated from birth until life closes / Hearts starve as well as bodies; Give us Bread, but give us Roses."
— "Bread and Roses," by James Oppenheim

The Gilded Age gave rise to a culture where there was no such thing as too much money. And in order to make more, many factory owners resorted to cutting costs and demanding even more from their employees. But these changes also led to a style of work and production that was ultimately unsustainable. Unsustainable for the workers, that is. Being a wealthy factory owner or manager, as we shall see, made for a pretty comfortable lifestyle, one that was built on the backs of other people, like the Triangle Factory girls. That large class of working people suffered mightily. They experienced illness, injuries, and even death.

HARD TIMES

Factory life in the early 1900s was no picnic. New York City factories employed thousands and thousands of workers to do repetitive and exceedingly boring labor that strained their muscles, their eyesight, and their patience. These workers, mostly young girls, worked six days a week for at least ten hours a day. For this work, they were paid no more than a few dollars a week. Girls sometimes even had to provide their own thread or other materials in order to complete their work. If they made a mistake—say, cut a piece of ribbon to the incorrect length—their paychecks would be docked, often for much more than the actual cost of the mistake.

Factory girls worked in squalid working conditions. If they were lucky enough to have a chair, it was often hard and backless. If a girl was fortunate enough to work near windows, she still might not see a ray of sunshine. Factories were often crowded with large machinery, while walls and windows were covered with yards of material. And on the off chance that windows were unblocked, they were obscured in grime, a result of a gritty city that exhaled smoke every second of every day.

A DAY IN THE LIFE OF ROSE COHEN

It's probably hard to imagine what a day in the life of a factory worker was like, but we do have oral histories that give us some idea.

Meet Rose Cohen. She survived the Triangle Factory fire and later shared her remembrances of her first factory job on Pelem Street in New York City.

It was the early 1900s, and Rose was just a teenager. Her family needed her to work, so school was not an option. One day, Rose's father found a job for her in a shop—a factory—where he knew the presser (the person who operated steam-pressing machines to iron the finished clothing). Rose was nervous about starting work, but she was excited too. She wanted to help her family. She wanted to feel growup. For many immigrant kids, or children of immigrants, holding paid employment was their initiation into adulthood.

Rose's father took her to the shop on the first day at seven in the morning. He advised her to show up at seven every morning in the hopes that the factory owner would not ask her to come earlier. Her father left her at the door and instructed her to work all day but to watch the clock. She should stand up and leave at 7 p.m. no matter what, regardless of what any other worker might do. "Be independent," he urged her.

"Yes, father," she replied, obedient as ever.

Rose carried with her a thimble, scissors, and two needles stuck in her coat lapel. She couldn't lose them, or she would have to buy new supplies out of her salary. For her breakfast, she brought a piece of bread that she'd eat later when nobody was looking. Rose went inside the factory, walking past the deafening roar of machines, until she found a man folding coats. "I am the new feller hand," she told him. (A feller hand is a person responsible for working on felled seams, a type of a sewing that uses a fancy topstitch.)

The man looked Rose up and down, surely taking in how young and inexperienced she appeared. "It's more likely that you can pull bastings than fell sleeve lining," he told her. Pulling bastings was far easier work and required no skill, though it was also less interesting and lower paid.

Rose understood that the man was questioning her skills. His doubt made her even more determined to show him that she could fell a seam with the best of them.

After some convincing, the man made space for her at a crowded table. He found her a chair, one with the back broken off so she wouldn't be able to lean back. She was so close to the other girls that she could probably feel their body heat. Summer heat, when it came, would make everyone miserable. For the moment, the factory was just stuffy and smelly.

Rose was given stacks of coats and instructed to work on the sleeves. It was better than pulling out bastings, but it was still repetitive work that was hard on her eyes and her body. But she had to get used to it. She would be doing it for twelve hours a day, six days a week. While she worked, she probably thought about that slice of bread—her breakfast—stuffed in her coat sleeve, wondering when she could take a break.

Even if she was allowed to talk to the girls around her, she wouldn't. They didn't like her right from that first day. They had been working longer and were faster than she, but she was at the same table with them right off the bat. Betsy, the head feller, snapped at her for taking too long and complained loudly to the others about Rose. "She's a strip of a girl coming and taking the very bread out of your mouth," Betsy said. Jobs were hard to come by, and Rose had gotten this one because of her father. She didn't know what to say to Betsy or the other girls, but she must have hoped that maybe they'd change their minds about her over time.

The presser kept watch over the girls to make sure they were not taking any breaks or wasting any time. The girls weren't even allowed a moment to stretch or to look out the window. Rose tried not to look at the presser, a man who had been a soldier. She'd been taught not to trust soldiers. He kept looking at her that first day, but she tried to ignore him. She didn't want to meet his eyes.

At 7 p.m., Rose was ready to go home, just as her father instructed. Her back was aching from sitting on that broken chair. But when she looked around, none of the other girls got up. They just kept working. In spite of what her father said, Rose waited until the others left. Everyone was miserable and hungry by then.

The next day Rose came back at 7 a.m. She hadn't even had a full twelve hours away from the shop. The shop boss stopped her at the door and told her she needed to be there earlier. Everyone was expected to work as long as he needed them to work. Keep in mind that Rose and the other girls were not being paid by the hour. They were paid a set rate, no matter how many hours they worked. Rose had no choice but to accept the terms of employment if she wanted to keep her job. She didn't want to disappoint her father, not after he went to the trouble of finding the job for her, and her family did need the money.

That evening Rose got up to leave when the other girls quit. The presser told her to sit down and finish one more coat. She was forced to finish even though the light was so dim she could barely see. She knew he was taking advantage of her because she was so young, but she had no recourse. What could she say? Nobody would take her side against a man.

At home Rose complained to her father about the presser and about how she had been treated at the shop. Rose's father didn't like it, but there wasn't much he could do to help her. If he marched down to the shop and ordered the presser to leave his daughter alone, she'd be fired. Besides, Rose's father worked from 5 a.m. to 11 p.m. He didn't have time to help Rose. He barely had time to sleep!

At the end of Rose's first week, she had worked more than sixty hours. She was bone tired, sore, and unhappy. And she took home $3, half of what the other girls were getting. It was not a lot of money, but it was enough to help her family. It was enough that she'd keep going back to the factory. Her father reminded her that she'd be able to get a better job with more experience. That seemed true. What Rose didn't know then was that she would eventually get enough experience to be hired at the Triangle Shirtwaist Factory. There she'd work a slightly shorter week and make friends with the other girls.

Until then, Rose got up and went to the crowded shop where the foreman made her work more than she was paid to work. She also missed her mother all day long. After all, she was still a kid.

A DAY IN THE LIFE OF SADIE FROWNE

Rose wasn't alone. All over New York City, young girls got up early to go to work. Sadie Frowne, for instance, woke up at 5:30 a.m. and had a cup of coffee and a slice of bread for breakfast, then left her apartment for the factory by 6 a.m. Once at the factory, she sat at her assigned table and received her the daily "stint," the pile of work she needed to complete before she could leave. Sadie was required to work until 6 p.m., but she'd have to stay even later if she couldn't finish. If she finished earlier, she'd be given more work, work that she would have to finish by quitting time or she'd have to stay late.

Sadie was good with a needle because she had lots of practice. Still, the days were long, and she got tired sitting at her table. When her eyelids drooped, she made mistakes. That's when the needle would go through her finger. She had to be careful not to bleed on the material, or she'd be responsible for paying for it out of her wages.

Unlike Rose, Sadie couldn't go home and tell her father about her day. Mr. Frowne died when Sadie was only ten years old, back when the family still lived in Poland. Mrs. Frowne, Sadie's mother, couldn't pay rent or buy food, so she brought her family to New York to live with her sister, Fanny. Sadie's mother was lucky enough to get a job right way. She worked long hours in a factory making "white goods" (a euphemism for underwear). Mrs. Frowne made $9 a week, but that was not enough for a family.

Sadie was too young for the factories, but Mrs. Frowne couldn't afford for her to stay home or go to school. So when she was thirteen, Sadie found a job as a house servant making $9 a month with room and board. She was happy enough with her job, and gave some of her money to her mother and saved the rest. But just when they were finding their footing, tragedy struck: Mrs. Frowne contracted consumption and died. Sadie used her savings to pay for her mother's funeral and burial.

With her mother gone, Sadie had to find better-paying work. That's how she ended up in a Manhattan sweatshop on Allen Street, with bleeding fingers and drooping eyelids. Every day she worked hard to keep her attention on the foot-powered machine. She knew she was always being watched.

Sadie kept a close eye on the clock when she was working because she was determined to leave by 6 p.m. Anything after was working for free. If she timed it right, Sadie would finish her last piece of the day just as the clock turned to six. Then she felt liberated, with her evenings all to herself. She could go dancing, go to the theater, or take a walk in the park if the weather was nice. At the end of each day, she would grab her coat and pocketbook and rush out of the factory. She'd take just a second or two to straighten her hair and smooth her dress. Outside, her boyfriend, Henry, would be waiting for her. Henry had asked to marry her several times already, but Sadie just laughed. She was not ready yet. She was still a young teenager with hopes and plans and dreams of her own.

She missed her mother, of course, but for the first time in her life, she had some spending money. She made $5 to $7 a week, which was not much, but enough. She dutifully put away at least $4 every week in her savings. The rest she used for food, rent, entertainment, and some new clothes every now and then. Oddly enough, Sadie was better off financially after her parents died because she only had to support herself.

This was partly because she shared a room and expenses with her roommate, Ella. They had a small oil stove in their kitchen for cooking, though their tastes were simple, usually canned vegetables, a bit of fruit, some meat, and bread. When they splurged, they drank tea and cocoa. They knew how to shop for bargains. Broken candy, for instance, was much cheaper than intact candy, and it tasted just as sweet. For ten cents a pound, they could have as much broken candy as they could stomach. They hated doing laundry, so they sent it out. It was worth the expense, they decided. Without laundry, they had more time to have fun.

Sadie and Ella agreed that they could be more frugal if they had to be. They could buy the half-rotten fruit or the old meat that had been on the shelf for too long. But they liked nicer things—fresh food, clean clothes, good fun. They thought nothing of spending a hard-earned dollar on a new shirtwaist. And, really, what was wrong with that? Sure, some of the older women criticized the girls and their spending. They said the girls shouldn't spend more than twenty-five cents a week on clothing, if that. But Sadie said those old women who criticized them were just "the old country people who have old-fashioned notions." The old ladies didn't get what it meant to be a modern girl in America.

Sadie's working life was hardly easy, and it wasn't always happy, either. But Sadie, like many girls her age, took tragedy in stride. Life was brutal; all the more reason to enjoy it where one could.

LIKE A PRISON SENTENCE

Girls like Rose and Sadie lived and worked all over New York City and made the best of their situations. They sometimes earned enough money to support themselves and have some fun in their limited off hours, like Sadie and her roommate Ella, but that was true only as long as they kept their jobs. If the factory boss decided he could hire someone with less experience for even less money, he would do it in a second. Sadie and Ella would then be out on the street, pounding the pavement looking for new jobs where they might have to work even more hours for less money. In the late 1800s, a person generally needed to make about $700 a year to ensure a basic standard of living, but most factory workers made only $400 or $500 a year.

Even if a worker could get by on her salary, she still had to worry about her safety at work. Take Rose Cohen, for example. After gaining experience at the small sweatshop, she moved up in position at the Triangle Factory, where she survived the 1911 fire, but only because she was luckier than hundreds of her coworkers. If she had been injured, she would have been out of work with no income. And if she had died, her family would have lost a paycheck they had come to depend on.

Even for workers who weren't injured or killed on the job, factory life was a bit like a prison sentence. As teens grew into adults, they needed more money and better job security, but factories did nothing to prepare anyone for a future beyond the walls of the factory. If anything, factory life ensured that these girls would never be anything but low-paid, badly treated, replaceable workers. From the perspective of factory owners, Rose, Sadie, and others like them were not people; they were cogs in the machine.

That vision of workers as disposable and interchangeable parts grew out of two important ideas about work and prosperity in the Gilded Age. First, employers believed that workers were expendable and therefore should be worked as hard as possible and as long as possible. The introduction of electricity in the late 1800s meant that factories could extend shift work. No longer would workers be sent home just because it was dark outside.

Second, employers believed that no single worker should ever have too much knowledge about the manufacturing process. Technological advancement made it easier to keep skilled human labor at a minimum. Prior to the late 1800s, for instance, sewing was an activity that required a skilled laborer. Tailors and seamstresses would make clothing from start to finish by hand. The introduction of industrial sewing machines meant that individual workers simply operated the machine.

Operating a sewing machine could be done by just about anyone, so factories could hire and fire at will. It didn't take long to train someone, and that worker could be replaced easily with anyone else who walked in the door and was willing to do the work for less money. People who had jobs had to be prepared to do absolutely anything to keep them. Those who entered the factory after apprenticeships or other training had to take lower-paying jobs because their skills were simply not useful. Imagine being a person in your late twenties or thirties who had spent years learning a craft. Mechanized factory work paid squat in comparison. What's more, you would likely be doing the same job as a fourteen-year-old.

TAYLORISM TAKES OVER

Frederick Winslow Taylor was a major reason why this shift toward repetitive, mechanized labor came about. Taylor completed high school at a prestigious school and was accepted at Harvard. He turned down the acceptance, however, because his eyesight was poor. He believed he'd damaged it from studying at night with bad lighting. (Taylor might have believed he damaged his eyesight, but studying in bad light will probably just give you a headache. It won't make you go blind.) With Harvard out of the equation, Taylor took a job at Enterprise Hydraulic Works in Philadelphia as an apprentice machinist. With his new skills, Taylor moved to Midvale Steel Company where he did a variety of jobs—from clerk to foreman to head engineer.

It was at Midvale where Taylor found his one true love: time and motion studies. It may be hard to believe that someone could love studying people work, but Taylor did. He watched people at Midvale Steel to see exactly how they were doing their jobs. He timed everything and then studied how he could change the factory setup and the workers' motions to eliminate any unnecessary movements. His recommendations did increase Midvale's efficiency, and Taylor decided he had a bright future ahead of him in the efficiency business. He started night school at Stevens Institute of Technology and earned a degree in mechanical engineering. In addition to efficiency work, he turned his attention to inventing. He eventually registered forty patents and left Midvale Steel to be a management consultant.

Taylor's legacy, however, was his time and motion studies. Based on the results, he created an industrial management system that influenced almost every major industry across the world. Known as Taylorism, his system broke factory jobs down to the absolute simplest and most efficient motions. In essence, Taylorism was a way of training humans to be more like machines.

Taylor saw himself as a workplace reformer, and he was much lauded for his work. And factories indeed became significantly more productive as a result of Taylor's insights. Henry Ford, the famed automaker, loved Taylorism. He based his entire factory practice on Taylor's work. But Taylorism came at a huge price for workers.

First, Taylor's system meant that all decisions were made by managers. Workers were expected to simply repeat motions without thinking; in fact, thinking got in the way. Taylor figured out that having to think made workers slower. The more they operated like machines, the more efficient they would be. His system ensured that no worker would ever have to make a decision.

A reprieve from thinking might not seem so bad. After a long day of making a million decisions and using your brain to solve tough problems, you might think that a mindless, repetitive job sounds kind of a nice. The reality is much harsher. Don't believe me? Well, go get a needle, a thread, a piece of material, and a button. Sew the button onto the material as fast as you can. It shouldn't take you more than a minute. Now do that 720 more times in the next twelve hours. You can get up once or twice to go to the bathroom, but you better be back in your seat within five minutes at the absolute most. Oh, and you'll be squeezed between two other people with barely enough room to move your elbows. Don't try to talk to your neighbors either, not even to ask a question. That'll slow you down. There'll be a foreman standing over you to make sure you don't even pause to gaze out the window. Good luck trying to breathe if it's August. It's going to be really hot. But in January, you'll have to learn to keep your fingers nimble because it'll be cold sitting there. Once you get good at sewing those buttons, you should be able to cut your time in half. After a few weeks on the job, your foreman will expect you to double your output. Now you'll need to sew 1,440 buttons a day. Keep moving! Buttons aren't going to sew themselves! You have to earn your $3 for the week.

Sounds terrible, right? You'd be lucky to get an "interesting" job like sewing buttons. Most factory workers spent their time with machinery and just pressed buttons or pulled levers.

Besides boredom, a second problem for workers was that Taylorism led to a lot of accidents. That's not surprising. People would grow so bored that they'd sort of zone out. Between 1880 and 1900, 35,000 people per year were killed on the job. Half a million people during that time were injured, some so badly that they were no longer able to work at all.

A third problem of Taylorism is that the system reduced the need for skilled workers—the system worked better if you could find highly unskilled workers. Workers who had some experience as apprentices or craftsmen were used to setting a routine and working at their own pace. They were accustomed to creating something from start to finish. They got to see the end product of their creative vision. Go back to the button-sewing example. I guarantee that you'll feel much more satisfied if you learn how to sew an entire shirt, rather than just sewing buttons on material. Humans aren't robots. We want to create. We want to think. We want to make use of our brains. But if you know how to sew the whole shirt, your knowledge might get in the way of your button sewing. For Taylor, it was better if you came to the factory with limited knowledge and stayed that way.

Under Taylorism, factory work became so easy to do (in terms of training) that children were able to do it. Between 1880 and 1900, children in cities all over America left school and went to work. By 1900, almost two million children under the age of sixteen were employed. (Compare that to 1880 when only 180,000 kids under sixteen worked.) Some states passed child labor laws to deal with the influx of child workers, but the laws weren't always enforced. The reality was that kids were cheap labor, and there was a seemingly endless supply of them. Taylorism meant that factory owners didn't have to train workers, so they could usher in a child of ten or eleven, show her which button to push, and then sit back and reap the financial rewards while giving the kid a measly few bucks. The absence of clear and enforced labor laws gave owners no incentive to ensure safety or protect workers from the exploitation or abuse in the workplace.

A fourth problem of Taylorism is that it dehumanized workers. The system assumed workers were dumb, apathetic, or lacking in creativity. Taylor advocated his system because he believed that immigrant workers who were unskilled and had poor English would benefit from simple work. In reality, Taylorism simply exacerbated immigrants' problems. Those who did lack skills were held back from developing any. Those who had poor English failed to develop better English because they weren't allowed to speak. Taylor didn't see a problem with this. (He was so enamored of his military-like systems that he even raised his kids by these principles!)

Unions, however, saw the inherent problems with a system that dehumanized workers—whether that was the intent or not. One labor leader summed it up like this: "No tyrant or slave driver in the ecstasy of his most delirious dream ever sought to place upon abject slaves a condition more repugnant." That was perhaps an exaggeration (and unfortunately dismissive of the very real horrors visited upon actual enslaved people just decades earlier), but studies showed that Taylorism did increase workplace stress, de-skill workers, and create long-lasting salary discrepancies between skilled and unskilled laborers. (Later studies showed that what workers benefited from was a sense of empowerment, something Taylor never even considered.)

Lest you think Taylorism is dead, that's certainly not the case. A recent study about a certain fast food chain in the United Kingdom showed that its managers largely accepted the principles of Taylorism, often operating with some engrained (and false) assumptions about how human beings work. For example, Taylorism requires an underlying acceptance that workers are inherently lazy and have to be monitored in order to stay on task. The philosophy assumes that workers need a hierarchical work structure where an immediate supervisor makes all the decisions. Taylorism assumes that there's only one right way to do things, and the job of the supervisor is to find that way and then force everyone else to work that particular method. It presumes that people work hardest if they are rewarded for output. The fast food study, and many others, show that these assumptions aren't necessarily true. Research suggests that what employees want most is fair pay, job security, and safety, along with a challenging work environment that rewards them for thinking.

THE LIFE OF A SHIRTWAIST

Because of Taylorism, most factory workers had no idea what happened beyond the steps they completed. The process for creating a shirtwaist was actually a long and involved set of steps that started well before the factory. The very beginning happened in a hot, wet cotton field somewhere in the South. Cotton had to be planted, tended, and picked—mainly by black workers who were exploited and mistreated to an even greater degree than the factory workers up north. From there, the cotton went where it could be spun and made into thread. After the threads were dyed different colors, only then could the thread be woven into material. These processes were completed by low-paid and overworked mill workers. The material they produced would be sold to a textile mill, and clothing manufacturers, like the Triangle Shirtwaist Factory, would then buy the cloth from the mill. Then the production process could begin.

Inside a factory like the Triangle Factory, workers would use a shirtwaist pattern made out of paper. (That meant lots of paper patterns were always floating around the factory. Talk about a fire hazard.) Cutters would then use a sharp tool to cut the fabric into different parts of the shirtwaist. In the early days of mass production, cutters used fabric shears to cut one measly layer of fabric at a time. Then an enterprising person invented a knife that could cut through sixteen layers of fabric. With an electric fabric cutter, factory workers could cut hundreds and hundreds of layers of cloth in a day.

Once the cutter had stacks and stacks of shirtwaist parts, he—usually men did the cutting—would call for someone to carry those parts to the appropriate section of the factory. (Before the rise of big factories in the early 1900s, cutting would have happened in a tenement sweatshop, and then a carrier, possibly a child, would have carried the parts to another sweatshop for the next step in the process.)

Once the cutters finished the fabric pieces, the basters in the factory would receive the parts. Basters were usually girls who would sit all day hand-sewing temporary stitches to hold the pieces of fabric together. The basters essentially created a mock-up of the shirtwaist. Then someone would carry the basted pieces to the sewers. The sewers would sew permanent stitches and remove the basting as they went. Early sweatshops required girls to sew by hand, but later, as factories adopted new technologies, machines were used instead. Girls would operate the machine by foot pedal while carefully guiding the fabric.

It's worth noting here that the sewing step in the shirtwaist life cycle moved far faster once factories became more mechanized. Isaac Singer invented the sewing machine in the 1850s, and once adopted by factories, it revolutionized clothing production. A hand-sewer could only do about thirty-five stitches a minute; but Singer's machine could do four hundred stitches a minute. That's more than eleven times faster than the hand-sewer!

Once a shirtwaist was permanently stitched, a worker would pick up the bundles and deliver them to the finishers, the next group of workers. They did all the finishing touches, like the buttons or embroidery work. Someone else would press the garment when it was done, using a big pressing machine. That was backbreaking work done in very hot conditions.

Other workers would inspect the shirtwaists as they were completed. If anything looked amiss, they would send the garment back for reworking. Someone else would sew a label in the finished piece. From there, the shirtwaists would go to shipping, where they were packed up and sent to stores. Only then could customers buy a shirtwaist. And they likely had no idea how many people it took to produce that one garment.

You probably noticed that all this work involved a lot of carriers. Freight elevators made it easier to transport pieces from one floor to another. Prior to the elevator, carriers simply loaded up as much fabric as they could on their backs and transported it as best they could.

FASTER BUT NOT ALWAYS BETTER

So why does Taylorism persist in spite of how bad it can be for workers? Sadly, the reason is because the system does often speed up production. And faster production for less money means that business owners and managers can make a lot more money. Employees and consumers can benefit too, if management is willing to pass on the financial windfalls. That's what Henry Ford did, at least in part. He debuted his Model T in 1908, and it was wildly popular. He had to find a way to produce the cars faster to satisfy demand. Six years later, he introduced what he called his "moving assembly line." It was a production line based on Taylorism and all of its attendant principles. Sure enough, Ford succeeded in making more cars even faster for less money: His assembly line made production a full 80 percent faster. A spiffy, new Model T used to take twelve and a half man-hours to produce; in an assembly line, workers could make a car in just two hours and forty minutes. Ford passed on the savings to his customers: A Model T produced the old way cost $575. With the new system, buyers could have a new car for just $345—a savings of $230.

So it's not that Taylorism is inherently bad. The problem is the people who apply the system without any care for the well being of workers. Somebody had to stand up for the rights of workers. But politics (and politicians) in the Gilded Age were so corrupt and generally unconcerned for human welfare that so many aspects of life then—from factory work to housing policy to the police force—were rotten to the core.

CHAPTER 7

CORRUPTION IN THE GILDED AGE

Among a people generally corrupt liberty cannot long exist.
—Edmund Burke

Every actual State is corrupt. Good men must not obey laws too well.
—Ralph Waldo Emerson

People like to talk about how corrupt politicians are. Listen to any talk radio program or watch a twenty-four-hour news station show, or eavesdrop on a group of political news junkies having coffee. Somebody in the conversation will call a politician crooked or say that he or she is a liar.

In some cases, the insult may be true. Other times, it's wild speculation. In the Gilded Age, though, politicians brought crooked to a whole new level. Some Gilded Age politicians were outright thugs who faced absolutely no consequences for their immoral and often illegal behavior. Thievery and deception were so common that people just expected it.

Some of the most corrupt people in the Gilded Age resided at Tammany Hall in New York. Named for a Delaware Indian chief called Tammanen, Tammany Hall became one of the biggest political machines of the time. The political organization—known as a machine in the metaphorical sense—was founded in the 1786 to oppose the Federalist Party. (The first boss was Aaron Burr, the legendary American historical figure best known for killing Alexander Hamilton in a duel.) Its primary purpose in the early days was to provide a forum for fraternal socializing. It was a place for the eighteenth-century elite to kick back, have a cup of whiskey or rum, and talk about their weird pantaloons. (Seriously, eighteenth-century pants were a little strange. Google them.) Tammany Hall became connected with the Democratic Party in the 1800s and was at its most influential between 1854 and 1934.

RAMPANT VOTER FRAUD

While Tammany Hall wasn't always a force for evil, it certainly seemed that way during parts of the Gilded Age. Powerful men in leadership positions, called bosses, convinced people to vote for candidates who supported Tammany Hall. The machine had a lot of strategies for swaying the vote, including paying people for their votes or promising favors. Sometimes Tammany Hall just gave out free beer. Illegal businesses that supported Tammany Hall—like bars and brothels—were allowed to stay open if the owners voted for the machine and then paid off the politicians who paid off the cops to look the other way. Tammany Hall handed out city contracts in exchange for favors, which meant that public works projects were often done slowly and poorly. The public couldn't trust that the people building their roads or constructing their bridges were the best people for the job. The builders were simply the people who could offer the best favors.

Tammany Hall's most notorious bosses fought any effort to reform their practices. They openly mocked reformers, which was bad enough. But they actively opposed any practice that would force them to clean up their act. For instance, one reform measure that voters pushed for was the secret ballot. It may be hard to believe, but the secret ballot is a recent invention. Early Americans voted out loud. They gathered in one spot, and each white man (black men didn't get the right to vote until 1870, and women didn't vote until the twentieth century) proclaimed his vote. The oral vote, as it was known, stuck around for a long time. The state of Kentucky, one of the last to change, kept it until 1891.

Even after most states had dumped the oral vote, the voting process certainly wasn't secret. The system in place during the Gilded Age had voters putting a colored slip of paper in a glass holder, each color representing a different candidate. Men would walk up to the glass holder and drop their slip of paper while everyone watched. The rationale for such a system is that even non-English speakers could vote since they didn't have to worry about reading a ballot. That might be true, but the colored paper system introduced even bigger problems. Tammany Hall would hire thugs to beat up anyone who voted for the wrong candidate. Even if you didn't get beat up, the political machine would use any form of intimidation to make sure you voted the way they wanted you to vote—otherwise you could lose your job, or worse.

Voter fraud was so common in the Gilded Age that it's a wonder anyone even bothered to vote at all, quite frankly. There were many ways an election could be tampered with that didn't involve blatantly beating up voters (and that certainly happened in plenty of elections). For instance, some districts didn't use the glass box method; instead, they asked voters to hand their ticket to a clerk. All it took was a few dollars in the clerk's hand if you wanted him to "lose" some of those particular tickets.

Fraudulent voting was a good way to make some extra cash. Whole jobs arose for anyone willing to commit fraud. For example, "colonizers" were voters who could be bought. The machine backing a candidate—if not the candidate himself—would find groups of colonizers and pay them to vote a particular way. A swath of colonizers could turn a whole election for what the machine considered small potatoes. It was easy money, and lots of people were very poor. They didn't have the luxury to think long term about the fact that they were voting for someone who was crooked enough to buy an election and would undoubtedly rob working-class citizens any chance they got.

"Floaters" were slightly more sophisticated than the colonizers. A floater would cast a ballot for the highest bidder. He'd move from party to party, depending on who paid him the most. If an election was close and votes were really critical, a floater could drive up the auction price and win a nice chunk of change for his work.

The most blatant of the vote fraudsters had to have been the "repeaters." They went from poll to poll, voting as many times as they could. They sometimes wore disguises and shamelessly handed ticket after ticket to the same poll worker, who believed he was collecting votes from different legitimate citizens!

Voter fraud was no secret, and Americans recognized the need for changes in the voting process. Citizens clamored for secret ballots. Though change was slow, it did happen. By 1892, thirty-eight states had instituted the secret ballot. No more glass boxes and colored tickets, and no more handing tickets to a clerk. While our lawmakers didn't completely eliminate voter fraud with the secret ballot, American citizens did send a powerful message to the political machines: They wanted a voice, and they wanted their voice to be heard without fear of retaliation.

TAMMANY HALL LEGENDS

Leaving aside these fraudulent voting practices for a moment, some immigrant voters really were loyal Tammany Hall supporters and chose to vote for its candidates of their own free will. That's because Tammany Hall politicians had a positive track record of helping the poor and immigrants. Tammany Hall provided legal assistance to those who needed it. It gave out free food on holidays for those who couldn't afford a Thanksgiving or Christmas dinner. It helped immigrants find jobs and fill out citizenship paperwork. People who had benefited from theses gratis services understandably voted for Tammany Hall politicians. To them, these politicians were heroes who were helping to make their American Dream a reality. Many voters honestly believed that the machine was serving their best interests. In reality, Tammany Hall mainly existed to benefit the fat cats who ran it. Yes, the politicians provided help to the poor, but they also created policies that systematically robbed those very same people.

BOSS TWEED

One of Tammany's fattest cats was a guy by the name of William "Boss" Tweed. Tweed was balding, portly, and cursed with out-of-control eyebrows. He became grand sachem (or leader) of Tammany Hall in 1868. He was eventually elected to New York State Senate, a post that he used to take over the New York City treasury with his political friends. He was so powerful that he eventually controlled all Democratic nominations for every city and county post. His habit of filling offices with friends who would look the other way when he broke the law was referred to as cronyism, a word we still use today to describe politicians who appoint their friends to key positions. Tweed and his cronies became known as the Tweed Ring. The Tweed Ring ended up costing American taxpayers a lot of money.

Tweed was a blatant and shameless crook. He opened a law office, even though he wasn't a lawyer, and charged for legal services. That law office was actually a cover for the money he was extorting from big companies, and if anyone questioned an influx of cash, he could point to his totally legal law firm. When he wasn't pretending to be a lawyer, he was stealing money in other ways. He and his cronies faked leases or made false vouchers or padded bills that they paid out of the city coffers. They essentially reached into the city bank account and took money for themselves while pretending to pay these fake bills. Tweed and his buddies stole so much that we aren't even sure what the total amount was. Some estimates suggest between $30 and $200 million by today's standards. That's a big range, and it demon-

William Marcy "Boss" Tweed

strates just how effective Tweed was at covering his tracks.

Tweed wasn't shy about flaunting his wealth. He was so powerful that nobody dared question him. Besides, anyone who worked closely with him was collecting money too, so everybody looked the other way as Tweed bought up property all over Manhattan and lived like a king. He even took to wearing a big diamond attached to the front of his shirt. That fashion choice was as tacky as it sounds, but Tweed didn't care; he wanted everyone to know he was filthy rich.

Not surprisingly, Tweed eventually got caught. He served two years in jail for larceny and forgery. Once out of jail though, he went right back to his thieving ways. He was caught again for embezzlement, but this time he decided to make a run for it. He went to Cuba and later to Spain, but he was found and extradited to the United States in 1876. He spent a year or so in jail before dying of pneumonia.

THE MASTER OF MANHATTAN

With Tweed dead, Tammany Hall could finally clean up its act. It could become a political force for good instead of a symbol of greed and immorality. That's not what happened, though. A few years after Tweed died, Tammany Hall got a new boss, Richard Croker. Known as the "Master of Manhattan," Croker was even more ruthless than Tweed. And he was smarter too.

Born in Ireland in 1843, Croker came to the United States when he was three years old. He attended public school in New York until he was thirteen, and then left and became an apprentice to a machinist. As a young man, Croker was a notorious street fighter who could hand out beatings with the best of them. (He even bloodied someone at a neighborhood picnic.) He was well known as a fighter, which is why Boss Tweed hired him to be a "shoulder hitter." That was someone who showed up at the polls and intimidated voters. One report suggests that Croker voted seventeen times in one election.

At some point, Croker met John Kelly, the new grand sachem of Tammany Hall after the fall of Boss Tweed. It was Kelly who helped Croker gain the skills, practice, and experience he needed to get into politics. In 1874 Croker ran for the position of coroner, which doesn't sound like a particularly impressive position. In New York, however, any city position promised spoils. Croker won the election, but he was charged with murder. Some reports suggest that he killed one of his enemies on election day. Other sources suggest that he killed someone in a street fight. Regardless, someone ended up dead, and Croker was charged with murder just as he was elected to an important political office. The trial ended with a hung jury, and Croker was never retried. He not only served as coroner for years, but also took over as grand sachem of Tammany Hall when Kelly died in 1886. For sixteen years, Croker ran Tammany with all the integrity of Boss Tweed—which is to say not very much at all.

Croker set an ambitious goal for himself when he took his position at the head of the Tammany Hall table. He decided that he would control all city posts. Not just a few key positions, like Boss Tweed, but all positions. Since there were about 90,000 city jobs at the time, that was a big goal indeed. It took him a few years, but he got very close. Because he eventually had almost every city job in his pocket, he could control everything that happened in the city. And because he had cronies everywhere, he never had to worry about getting caught doing the many unethical things he did. To give just a couple of examples: He created a real estate company, which he used to sell property to the city government, and he bought financial interests in various companies and then awarded them city contracts. Both activities were highly suspect, given that they represented a huge conflict of interest. But Croker was smart. He didn't do anything obviously illegal, and he had friends and allies everywhere. He had a knack for avoiding prosecution.

With all those city contracts, Croker was rolling in the dough. He had a Fifth Avenue mansion in Manhattan. He had racehorses and vacation homes in the United States, Ireland, and English. He was worth millions of dollars.

By 1902, however, Americans were getting sick of Tammany Hall. While government cronies prospered under corrupt leadership, regular Americans were fighting to keep their jobs and put food on their tables.

The factory workers were trying to make their way in a political and economic environment that had been stacked against them for years. It's not surprising that voters became so fed up that they voted Croker out of office. He took all his money—earned on the backs of working Americans—and moved to Ireland, where he lived a life of leisure until 1922, eleven years after the Triangle disaster.

A TIME TO FIGHT

Though not directly responsible for the fire, Croker and Tweed and their cronies were responsible for fostering a climate of greed that harmed a lot of people. But one good thing came out of this time period, and that was a new class of workers who were determined to fight back.

As a direct result of Tammany Hall and other unethical and illegal practices, ordinary Americans mobilized into unions. Those unions became a force for major changes in the way working-class Americans lived and worked. Much of the union mobilization happened as a direct result of women—often immigrants—who for the first time began to participate publicly in politics.

As we'll see later, certain groups of people today still work in deplorable conditions. And the wealthiest few still control a small number of enormous corporations that are worth billions of dollars. But workers in America do have rights. Rights that didn't come easily. Rights that we have because people were willing to fight for them, often at the expense of their own lives. We owe a debt to all those workers, including the Triangle Factory workers and others just like them.

Isn't it funny to think that our safety at work today is possible because a group of immigrants, many of them teenaged girls, fought for us? But that's exactly what happened.

CHAPTER 8
UNION GIRLS

If I went to work in a factory the first thing I'd do is join a union.
— Franklin D. Roosevelt

I am glad to see that a system of labor prevails under which laborers can strike when they want to.
— Abraham Lincoln

Factory girls made the best of their situation because they had no other choice. They counted small blessings: They were grateful that factory life was better than life in the tenement sweatshops, the workspaces that existed prior to factories. Factories had better light and better ventilation (not that either was particularly good, but everything is relative). Factories also had bathrooms, and the workers could take a minute or so to use the facilities occasionally. That wasn't great, but at least they could pee once or twice in a twelve-hour day.

A girl's experience in a factory largely depended on how humane the factory owners were. Unfortunately, many of the factory owners were driven primarily by greed and weren't particularly kind to their workers. Let's say a girl forgot to bring her lunch one day. She could at least get a drink of water at work, right? Nope. Some factory owners charged a couple of cents for a glass of water and a piece of dry cake. Some bosses believed that the girls worked harder if they yelled at them constantly. Sometimes the owners even charged girls rent on a chair or for a locker to store her pocketbook, coat, and hat. Some girls had to pay for the electricity they used to run their sewing machines, and could be fined for speaking to each other on the job. Arriving a few minutes late at work, even once, could cost a girl half a day's pay, even though she worked all but five minutes of the day. Unscrupulous bosses might even mess with the clock. During lunch, they'd speed it up so the girls got a shorter break. And around quitting time, they'd set the clock back so girls had to work even longer—without pay.

As you've already read, there wasn't much the workers could do to fight back. With so many immigrants arriving, owners could easily fire people and hire the next group of immigrants—sometimes for even less pay.

Even though organizing and protesting unfair labor practices often led to being fired or worse, brave people all over New York City (and beyond) decided to stand up and fight in the form of organized unions. And unions really did scare the factory owners, especially when they were led by driven and charismatic people. Clara Lemlich was one such leader.

CLARA LEMLICH

Clara Lemlich was born in Gorodock, Ukraine, in 1886. While her Jewish father studied scriptures, she and her mother supported the family. Clara was eager to learn, so she raised money by writing letters for her illiterate neighbors who had family in America. When she wasn't writing letters or working, she learned to sew buttonholes, a good way to make a bit of extra cash. Clara used her extra money to buy novels. She loved Tolstoy, Turgenev, and Gorky. Her father, however, hated Russia and the anti-Jewish czars, so when he found Clara's novels, he threw them out. That probably upset Clara, but she didn't let it stop her. She simply bought more novels (and probably found better hiding places).

In 1903 Clara's father brought the family to America. Like the other eastern European immigrants we have already met, Clara found work in a factory, the Gotham Shirtwaist Factory, just two weeks after she arrived in America. Gotham treated its employees dismally. Clara, at the age of seventeen, worked sixty-six hours a week for about $3. That meant she was getting paid about four-and-a-half cents per hour. (In today's economy that translates to about $1.20—well below the now federally mandated minimum wage.) Clara was understandably livid. Factories, she wrote, had reduced workers to "machines."

By 1909 she had found work as a draper at Louis Leiserson's shirtwaist factory. As a draper, Clara would look at a shirtwaist design on paper and then create the look by arranging—or draping—fabric on a dummy to create the actual garment. Draping required real skill, which meant it paid a little more than a regular factory job. She wasn't rich by any means; she wasn't even well paid. But her position did give her a little extra money to pursue her education. She spent a lot of her time in the library reading or going to classes, where she studied Marxist theory. She also attended union meetings.

Clara joined the International Ladies' Garment Workers' Union (ILGWU) to fight the injustices of factory life. Though she made a decent wage, most of her coworkers didn't. And they all suffered the indignities of factory life—the one-minute bathroom breaks, the managers who yelled at them and who messed with the clocks to get free work, the nightly searches before the girls could pass through the locked doors, and all the other reminders that factory workers were barely human. Fed up with factory bosses, Clara and a few other ILGWU members formed a union group called Local 25. Through sheer persuasion, Clara and her friends managed to add about forty more members to Local 25. Most were other girls who worked in dress or shirtwaist factories. Male factory workers largely ignored the group. They had their own union groups and weren't particularly interested in what a group of young girls were doing. But Clara was committed to keeping Local 25 going because she was determined to improve working conditions in the factories, no matter what the cost.

Strikes were common in the early 1900s, and Clara was no stranger to them. In 1907 she organized a strike at Weisen and Goldstein's in Manhattan, a shop considered a model factory at the time. It was modern and spacious, not at all like the cramped and dark basements of the older sweatshops. The tradeoff, however, was that a modern factory meant mechanized production and increasingly difficult production targets. Workers were made to work faster and faster. As soon as they hit one goal, they were pushed to meet another, higher target. Clara led what was known as a wildcat strike, a walkout at one shop as opposed to organized strikes at multiple garment factories. The Weisen and Goldstein strike lasted ten weeks. That meant ten weeks of delayed production for the factory and significant motivation for the owners to make changes.

In 1908 Clara also led a walkout at the Gotham factory. The owners were firing higher-paid, skilled workers and hiring women or children at lower wages. That was exactly the kind of shady business practice that was totally legal but which Clara and other trade unions protested—often successfully.

By 1909 Clara was becoming something of an expert at leading strikes. She was working at Leiserson's on West Seventeenth Street in Manhattan, after having been fired from two previous jobs for leading strikes. By this time she had developed a reputation as a rabble-rouser, but Leiserson hired her anyway, perhaps because he shared some of her socialist ideas. He was also from eastern Europe and had worked his way up in factories to open his own shirtwaist shop. While Leiserson seemed sympathetic to workers, Clara became sorely disappointed in him after he broke his promise to hire only union workers and secretly hired nonunion workers at his newly opened second shop. A group of skilled laborers—all men—met to discuss what to do. Clara broke into the meeting uninvited and argued that any strike must include the women workers as well, that the men needed the women in order to make Leiserson feel the sting of a strike. She got her wish when everyone joined the strike. Leiserson was forced to make concessions in order to get his workers back on the job.

The summer of 1909 was a humdinger for strikers. Clara's knack for rallying workers, with the help of other leaders who were fed up with factory conditions, led to massive walkouts. Those walkouts happened because Clara and her colleagues were instrumental in helping workers understand the importance of strikes.

As a union man once said to Clara: When a bottle of milk is produced, the owner is in control of the entire process—from buying the milk from a dairy farmer to bottling it, labeling it, and selling it in a store. All along the way, workers contribute to that process, but they see none of the profit. They don't even get any of the milk. That analogy struck a chord with Clara, and she started talking about shirtwaists in the same way. All over the city, bosses controlled the production of garments. No matter how hard workers toiled, they didn't see the profits. Yet the shirtwaists wouldn't exist without the workers. That idea lit a fire under the people who had been told their whole working lives that they existed to serve someone else's interests.

In July garment workers at Rosen Brothers. walked off the job because they wanted a 20 percent raise. Keep in mind that these workers weren't whining. They were being paid a wage that was almost impossible to live on, and they were being abused in the process. In response, Rosen Brothers. hired strikebreakers, thugs who intimidated strikers—often through violence. Naturally, the Tammany Hall police sided with management because workers had no kickbacks to offer; Rosen Brothers. management, however, had all kinds of money to buy people off. In spite of aggressive strikebreakers and crooked police, workers at Rosen Brothers. held their strike for a month. Management realized they needed to start producing again in time for their busy season, so they relented and gave the pay increase.

In August of 1909, New York witnessed a huge walkout by workers in the neckwear industry. Seven thousand of these workers walked out of factories and sweatshops across the city and stayed out for a month. That might not seem like much, but remember that these people didn't get paid for a month, and they had no idea how long they would have to strike. It would have been easier just to go back to work. But they stuck together, all seven thousand of them. They were hungry and scared, but they knew that they would never see changes if they didn't

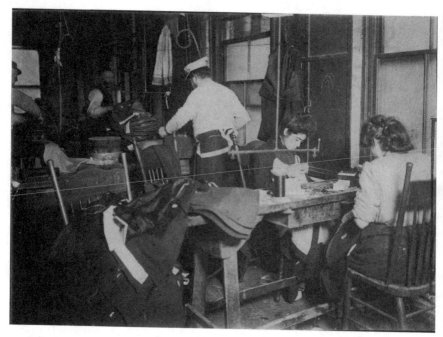

Workers at a tenement sweatshop on Suffolk Street in Manhattan, 1908.

make the factory owners feel financial pain.

Their demands were eminently reasonable. Many of these girls were working in cramped, unventilated tenement basements, and sometimes even tenement bedrooms. They wanted to put an end to that practice. Owners needed to be able to provide safe workspaces. And workers needed to be paid fairly for the hours they worked.

After a month, the owners of these factories and sweatshops started to get a little nervous. They didn't expect the girls to hold out as long as they did, and there was no sign that they were stopping. The owners felt like they had no choice, so they agreed to negotiate. The workers got some of what they asked for. The strike wasn't an unqualified success in that regard, but it was important because it showed what workers could do when they banded together behind a common cause.

Clara Lemlich knew how powerful united groups could be, and

she was instrumental in helping people mobilize. That is precisely why a man by the name of Charles Rose was hired to beat her up. Yup, you read that right. Clara was working on a strike at a Fifth Avenue factory, and her earlier successes had a lot of owners and managers scared. Charles Rose seemed to be the perfect means for taking her out. If Rose did his job well, Clara would be too scared to continue.

On Friday evening, September 10, 1909, Clara was walking down to the Lower East Side in Manhattan. Where she was going was not clear, but it was probably to the library, one of her classes, or the union hall. She was dressed like many young girls of the time who participated in the unions and labor strikes, in a long skirt, a blouse, and a necktie. Many of the women wore men's neckties, probably to underscore that they were working in a man's world. Some female labor activists even cut their hair short, like men, to signify their rebellion.

Charles Rose followed behind her from a distance. He was pretty sure he could corner her and beat her up on his own, but he'd enlisted the help of a colleague just in case. That colleague was a ne'er-do-well by the name of William Lustig. Rose and Lustig, dressed in dark suits and derby hats, skulked behind an unsuspecting Clara.

At some point, Clara turned around and spotted the men lurking. She knew exactly who they were because she'd seen them at picket lines, but there was nothing she could do because they were too close to her and she had nowhere to run. Rose and Lustig moved in. The beating was quick and brutal. When they were done, Rose and Lustig left Clara bruised and bleeding on the street.

Clara was badly beaten and had several broken ribs, and Rose and Lustig were certain she'd be too frightened to resume her labor-organizing activities. But they didn't know Clara. After a few days at home to recover, Clara went back to the garment district—and now she was really angry. It was time, she argued, for the entire garment district to go on strike. Rose and Lustig—and the cowards who had hired them—were floored. It seemed that nothing could stop Clara Lemlich from fighting.

UNIONS FIGHT FOR WORKERS' RIGHTS

Unions began to pop up all over the United States in response to abuses of power by factory owners. The best known was the Noble and Holy Order of the Knights of Labor. (You have to admit that's a pretty impressive name.) The Knights were a collection of unions with thousands of members. By 1886, the same year Croker took over Tammany Hall, the Knights had thousands of members in each of its many unions. The main organization boasted a total of 700,000 members. That's a little more than the population of Seattle, Washington, today!

The Knights were against laissez-faire capitalism, the prevailing ideology of the time. Laissez-faire capitalism meant the government tried to keep from interfering in business endeavors. The idea behind it was this: If individuals were left to pursue their own best interests, they would naturally create the best circumstances and outcomes for all of society. Government regulation would simply hamper individuals' abilities to reach their desired ends. Thus, the job of government in a laissez-faire economy is simply to keep order and enforce contracts.

Here's an example of how laissez-faire capitalism can be problematic and dangerous. Suppose you have a lemonade stand. Free from government intervention and regulation, you can set your stand up quite easily and quickly. That sounds good so far. But then suppose you figure out that you can make more money if you buy cheaper cups in which to serve your customers lemonade; in fact, you can save 30 percent on your overhead costs if you serve lemonade in cups that you buy from a factory overseas that uses a newfangled kind of material that's far cheaper than plastic. Now suppose that you can cut costs even more if you reduce the sugar you put in the lemonade by half and you use a much cheaper sweetener that your friend makes in his chemistry lab. Once again, the customers don't mind because they don't know, and you are making more money than ever. But what happens if it turns out that the cups you are supplying contain some kind of dangerous residue from the material that causes a horrible disease in people who drink from them? And what if the artificial sweetener made in your friend's lab causes cancer? You might have known these things if you'd done some research, but you didn't take the time. You were too focused on maximizing your profit. If regulations had been in place, the government agency responsible for overseeing lemonade stands would have told you that you needed to know what was in that cup material and in the sweetener. Regulations would have ensured that you couldn't use anything that wasn't proven safe for consumers. Sure, it would be great if every lemonade stand proprietor thought about health and safety first, but that's not how humans work. Without intervention, even the best people may cut corners to maximize profits without considering long-term consequences for the public.

So the problem with laissez-faire capitalism, as the Knights soon figured out, was that it failed to predict all the ways that humans, in the process of pursuing their own best interests, would trample on the rights and interests of other humans. Factories in the 1800s and early 1900s provided ample evidence that owners couldn't be trusted to pursue their own ends without abusing workers. Factory workers needed laws that would protect them. And that's exactly what the Knights fought for.

While unions, then and now, have been accused of being anti-capitalist, that certainly is not always the case. The Knights and many of the other unions that sprouted up in response to the legacy of Gilded Age economics didn't oppose capitalism at all. They simply opposed the abuses that an overly empowered ownership could inflict on its workers. The Knights and other unions fought for equal pay for men and women. They fought for an eight-hour workday for all workers. They opposed child labor. They wanted safety measures in place for all workers. They served as the voice of those who couldn't speak out on their own behalf.

With thousands of workers mobilized, the Knights began launching strikes. From 1880 to 1900, the Knights were responsible for 37,000 strikes, many of which changed workplace policies to benefit and protect workers. Eventually, the Knights of Labor split up, but what arose instead was a long-lasting and influential labor union, the American Federation of Labor (AFL). By 1904, the AFL had 1.5 million members.

ON STRIKE

Labor union membership required workers to participate in strikes, something that wasn't always easy. Strikes came with a huge price attached for workers. For one thing, workers didn't get paid while on strike. Unable to feed their families and pay rent, strikers were highly motivated to cross the picket lines and go back to work. Keep in mind that in the early 1900s there were no government social services to help the poor. There was no safety net. If you didn't get paid, you and your children didn't eat. The lack of social support is part of why Tammany Hall was so influential. It stepped in to help loyal workers, but didn't take kindly to anyone who protested unfair labor policies.

Even worse than elimination of a wage was the violence that happened on picket lines. Between 1870 and 1914, between five hundred and eight hundred striking workers lost their lives. Most of those deaths were caused by the military, the state militia, or local police. Even if strikers weren't killed (and most weren't), they faced violence from street toughs hired by factories owners and political machine bosses. An organization called the Greater New York Detective Agency existed to offer strikebreakers for a range of services (not excluding violence). In 1909 the agency even sent letters to factories advertising strikebreaking work. It often offered replacement workers if necessary, which meant that factory owners didn't have to completely halt production during strikes.

Freelance toughs, like Charles Rose and William Lustig, also offered their services. These hired guns were often called shtarkers, Yiddish for "tough guys." Shtarkers would hang out around picket lines and beat up anyone they could corner. For that, shtarkers made a few dollars. For $100 or more, they'd murder someone. (And Clara Lemlich was so dangerous to factory owners that it's a wonder she wasn't killed.)

Strikers didn't have the support of the police or of the courts. A striker could be sent to do hard labor at a workhouse on Blackwell's Island (now known as Roosevelt Island) in the East River in New York City. There, inmates were given nothing but moldy bread and tepid water for meals and had to wash with lye soap, which burned the skin. They weren't allowed to talk to each other for fear they would plan an uprising. If the prisoners talked or failed to finish their work or committed some other infraction, they had to spend the night in what amounted to a dungeon full of rats. All of that just for going on strike to protest unfair labor practices!

Instead of being outraged by these practices, many judges believed the workers got what was coming to them. A man by the name of Judge Olmstead told strikers exactly what he thought of them: "You are on strike against God and nature, whose firm law is that man shall earn his bread in the sweat of his brow. You are on strike against God." Can you imagine what it was like to hear these words? Workers were told that they were fighting God's will—God's will that they should work in factories where owners constantly cheated them out of wages and treated them like animals rather than humans. If the judge's words didn't shame workers, the factory owners had another idea. At one factory, the owner brought in a priest to talk to strikers. This factory employed Italian immigrants who were devout Catholics. The priest—probably paid by the factory owner—told the workers that striking was against God's will. If the threat of violence or hard labor didn't work, the threat of God's disapproval from the mouth of a priest probably did.

Fortunately, some influential people were willing to help the union cause. Activists who called themselves the Women's Trade Union League (WTUL) rallied around workers, providing finan-

William English Walling, founder of the WTUL

cial, emotional, and tactical support. WTUL was founded in 1903 by William English Walling, a wealthy man from Kentucky. Walling was concerned about young girls being pushed into prostitution, a job that might have seemed better than the squalid factory conditions and the unlivable wages. Walling garnered the support of influential women all over the East Coast, including Eleanor Roosevelt. WTUL members would show up in the garment district a few days a week with giant banners encouraging workers to organize.

The Gilded Age years of the late 1800s, a time when wealth seemed endless for the few white men who made a grab for it, led to a nation-wide reform movement on behalf of workers. From leading voices in factory reform came union leaders, individuals who were sick of working to line the pockets of people like Tweed and Croker, the crooked politicians running New York. Unions became the voice of the people.

CHAPTER 9

TRIANGLE FACTORY ON STRIKE

Every man is dishonest who lives upon the labor of others, no matter if he occupies a throne.

—Robert Green Ingersoll

Poor and restricted are our opportunities in this life; narrow our horizon; our best work most imperfect; but rich men should be thankful for one inestimable boon. They have it in their power during their lives to busy themselves in organizing benefactions from which the masses of their fellows will derive lasting advantage, and thus dignify their own lives

—Andrew Carnegie

One of the most influential labor support groups came from an unlikely collection of members: rich white women. Known as the Mink Coat Brigade, they helped strikers mobilize. The group was co-founded by Alva Belmont, a wealthy widow of a banker. Her signature look was a long black skirt, a black hat with a feather in the brim, and a black fur muff. She might have been a society lady, but Belmont was no shrinking violet. She would spend nights at the Jefferson Market Court and bail out strikers as they were brought in.

VOICES FOR REVOLUTION

Other Mink Coaters included Anne Morgan, daughter of the banking titan J. P. Morgan. Born in 1873, Anne grew up extremely wealthy. She had the best education money could buy, slept in a mansion, and could indulge in whatever struck her fancy. But rather than throwing huge parties and draping herself in furs, Anne decided to help the garment workers. Along with several of her wealthy friends, Anne marched on the picket lines, believing that strikebreakers and police would be less likely to attack strikers if they were surrounded by members of high society. That would make for very bad press for the factory owners. Anne and the other Mink Coaters spent thousands of dollars bailing strikers out of jail and worked tirelessly to bring lawsuits against crooked police officers.

In late September of 1909, just three weeks after thugs beat up Clara Lemlich, Local 25—along with the Mink Coat Brigade, the ILGWU, and the WTUL—led Triangle Factory workers on a strike. By November 22, 1909, about half of Triangle's workers were still on strike. Local 25 called a meeting to discuss labor issues citywide. Thousands of workers attended this meeting, packing into the Great Hall at Cooper Union, just blocks away from the Triangle Factory. The workers listened as labor activists from all walks of life talked about labor policies, unions, and organizational strategies.

As she listened, Clara started to worry that the meeting would end with no plan, and she didn't have patience for the endless talk. So Clara stood up and delivered a speech in Yiddish that included these words: "I am a working girl, one of those who are on strike against intolerable conditions. I am tired of listening to speakers who talk in general terms. What we are here for is to decide whether we shall strike or shall not strike. I offer a resolution that a general strike be declared now."

When Clara finished speaking, people stood up and cheered.

PAULINE NEWMAN

One member of the audience that night was Pauline Newman, just a teenager herself. Before coming to America in 1901, Pauline lived in

Lithuania. There she was barred from attending a public school because she was Jewish and poor. So she fought to attend a Jewish boys' school—and she won.

Pauline's father died in 1901, and the family had no way to support itself, so they came to New York to make their living. Pauline was eight years old when she started her first job at the Triangle Shirtwaist Factory. She worked seventy-two hours a week for a total of $1.50. That's just two cents an hour! Pauline's working conditions would have been abominable for anyone, let alone for an eight-year-old.

In the few hours when Pauline wasn't working, she attended the Socialist Literary Club, where she learned about progressive economic and social theories. It was there that she improved her English. By 1907 she had joined a trade union and was participating in strikes. By 1909, she was so influential in labor politics that the Socialist Party selected her as its candidate for New York secretary of state. She was just sixteen! Imagine that. Most sixteen-year-olds now are just thinking about getting their first jobs. Pauline was working on changing the face of American labor.

Pauline quit the Triangle Factory before the fire because she didn't have time to work in a factory when she was spending all her days and nights fighting for justice. She was in the room that November day when Clara stood up and called for a massive strike. She agreed with Clara: Something had to be done to address the plight of immigrant factory workers in America.

Before calling a vote, labor organizers warned the crowd to think carefully. A strike would mean great hardship for everyone in the room. They would be hungry and cold. Their families would suffer. They had to be prepared to follow through as long as it took, even if it was months and months. The crowd listened carefully, and then they voted. They overwhelmingly voted yes. Together the workers took a Yiddish oath: "If I turn traitor to the cause I now pledge, may this hand wither from the arm I now raise." They meant business.

The next day was a Tuesday, a typical workday. But instead of working, 15,000 New York City garment workers walked off the job. Clara and her supporters, including Pauline, had not just started a strike; they had started a revolution.

ROSE PERR

Rose Perr was a sixteen-year-old sewing machine operator at the Bijou Waist Company. On that first day of the strike, Tuesday, November 23, 1909, Rose showed up at work, wondering how the strike would proceed. She'd heard the news that Local 25 had organized a massive walkout, but she wasn't sure what it would look like. She sat down at her sewing machine, as on any other day, and waited quietly with her coworkers. The girls kept their hats and coats nearby, ready to make an exit as soon as they were given some kind of signal. But no signal came.

As the girls sat at their machines, they whispered to each other about what would happen next: "Shall we wait like this?" "There is a general strike." "Who will get up first?" "It would be better to be the last to get up, and then the company might remember it of you afterward and do well for you." But Rose responded, "What difference does it make which one is first and which one is last?" Rose was right. Companies were rarely loyal to workers under any circumstances. For two hours the girls debated about what to do.

Finally, Rose couldn't stand it anymore. She stood up. When she looked around, she saw that her colleagues were standing up too. They put on their hats and coats, reached for their handbags, and then filed out together. That must have been a sight for management to see. Here were all their workers marching out the door, leaving the machines idle and the floors empty.

Outside the factory, Rose was frightened to see the police lined up. They held clubs and threatened the girls if they got out of order. The girls huddled together, wondering what to do next. Someone suggested they go right to the source—the union leaders. One of the girls knew how to use a telephone—yes, there was a time when not everyone knew how to use the phone—and she called the union. The union volunteer who answered the phone instructed the girls to go directly to one of the many temporary meeting halls being set up around the city. Volunteers at the local unions were trying to find meeting spaces to hold strikers. The volunteers had been told to expect five thousand strikers, but three times that number walked out. They had to work like crazy to get everything organized.

Once safely situated at a meeting space a few blocks away, the factory girls were told to write down their demands. Rose later realized that the union organizers wanted to occupy them for a bit while they figured out next steps. The unions had already made their demands of the factory owners. Still, Rose and her colleagues discussed what they wanted and scratched these demands out on paper. It's heartbreaking to read that list now because what Rose and her friends wanted are the very things that we expect to have in any job. Their demands included fair pay for their work. They wanted their wages to be set by a committee, not by the whims of their bosses. They wanted shorter hours (no more fourteen-hour shifts). They didn't want to be forced to work through the night. If night hours were necessary due to market demand, they wanted those hours scheduled in advance and compensated. And they wanted better treatment from management. That meant no more yelling at them, threatening them, or harassing them.

Eventually, after hours in the meeting space, the union organizers sent Rose and her friends home. But they were told to return to the Bijou Waist Company the next morning. The girls would picket from 7:45 a.m. to 9:30 a.m. As shops opened, everyone would see the strikers marching with their banners. At 5:15 p.m., the girls were to return to march as the shops closed. In between, Rose and the other girls would march in the streets downtown, carrying banners and chanting.

On the first day of the strike, Rose showed up at the appointed time. She was surprised to see a group of Italian strikebreakers arrive by automobile. Nobody came to work in a car. It was simply unheard of. But here they were: strikebreakers being dropped off by automobiles, hired by factory managers. Strikebreakers, or scabs, worked against the unions. Rose and everyone else must have felt scared and worried when they saw those workers. The girls knew what would happen to them if scabs simply took their place in the factories—the owners would have no incentive to change their ways.

THE UPRISING OF THE 20,000

What Rose and other strikers didn't know is that this strike was about to become a labor walkout so big that it would be talked about for years to come. The same day factory owners hustled scabs into the factory, five thousand more workers went on strike, including cutters. Cutters were skilled laborers who made higher factory wages than any other workers and could not be easily replaced. More workers walked out all day. By close of business, 20,000 garment district workers from five hundred shops around New York were on strike. For the first time, factory workers had the upper hand. There was absolutely no way that factory owners would find 20,000 people to replace those workers.

Clara was there throughout the strike. On that first day, she stood up and spoke to the strikers, including Rose. "We know that if we stick together—and we are going to stick—we will win!" she cried. She was right to be optimistic. In just two days, seventy owners of smaller shops caved. They needed their workers back on the job, and they agreed to all the demands—a 20 percent pay increase, a fifty-two-hour workweek, and union bargaining power.

TRIANGLE FIGHTS BACK

The larger shops, however, had no intention of giving in so easily. They were ready to fight their workers, no matter what the cost. At the Broadway Central Hotel, a group of twenty factory owners, including the Triangle Factory's Max Blanck and Isaac Harris, met to discuss their options. All the owners agreed that the sooner they ended the strike, the better, but absolutely nobody was prepared to give in to unions. They knew that a strong union would forever put the owners in a position where they would need to constantly respond to workers' demands. The owners agreed to start their own group, a collection of owners who could work together when responding to unions. As was the fashion at the time, they gave themselves a very long and hard-to-remember name: Allied Waist and Dress Manufacturers Association (AWDMA). The group agreed that they would resist the strikers as long as they could. They hoped that their resistance would once and

Strikers on the picket line during the uprising of the 20,000.

for all crush the unions. Every person in the room signed a declaration of "no surrender."

Half of the Triangle workers had been on strike since September, yet the factory was still producing shirtwaists. Blanck and Harris tried to keep their remaining workers satisfied so they wouldn't join the strike. To that end, they put a Victrola on the ninth floor and invited workers upstairs for dance contests at lunchtime. They awarded prizes for the best dancers and served oranges, rolls, and tea to their employees. The fine treatment might have fooled some workers, but the half or more on strike didn't buy that such good treatment would last after the strike. Blanck and Harris were already working on a plan to relocate the factory to Yonkers, north of New York City, where they would be beyond the reach of unions. Treating employees to dance contests and free food was just a way to placate workers until the unions were gone.

THE MINK COAT BRIGADE PARADE

The strikers knew they just had to hold on. And they did. On December 21, 1909—a month after the strike began—the Mink Coat Brigade staged a parade of automobiles driven by uniformed chauffeurs down Fifth Avenue in Manhattan. The ladies rode in the cars and carried banners in support of the Triangle strikers. *The New York Times* ran an article with the headline blaring, "Rich Women's Aid Gives Strikers Hope." Beneath the headline are the words, "Shirtwaist Girls Sure of Victory Since Miss Morgan and Others Joined Their Cause." (Notice how the headline credits rich women for their contributions. The workers themselves were sacrificing almost everything to participate in the strike, yet the newspaper didn't give them nearly as much credit.)

In early 1910, the Triangle owners started to waver. Blanck and Harris knew they couldn't go much longer without a full workforce. For that reason, they agreed to make some concessions. They announced that they would offer higher wages and reduced working hours.

You might think the strikers would have been overjoyed. Some probably were. But they refused the offer. They had to. Because Triangle was one of the largest shops in town, everybody was watching to see what kind of deal they would strike. The workers knew that their most important demand was the one that allowed them to unionize, and they wouldn't accept any deal, no matter how good it was, unless they could freely form unions without fear of being fired for doing so. (As it stood, members of unions feared exactly that.) Blanck and Harris refused, largely because they were worried unions would provide too much power to workers. The strikers stayed on the picket lines. Almost three months into the strike, and there was simply no end in sight.

At that point, around January of 1910, Anne Morgan of the Mink Coat Brigade withdrew her support of the strikers because she was against union organization, a practice she thought constituted socialism. It's a complicated issue, but the fact is that unions are not signs of socialism per se. But unions at the time were often associated with socialism, a movement people feared would displace capitalism and threaten the economic order of the United States. Union-phobes were right to be afraid. While unions didn't usher in socialism, they did give great power to workers, power that the owners wanted for themselves.

THE LONG WINTER OF 1910

You may think the strikers were being petty by holding out. But remember that refusing a deal was much harder than accepting one. They'd been out of work for months. They had no money and no idea how much longer they would have to strike. Accepting a partial deal would have felt like success, even if it wasn't exactly what they wanted. It must have been very tempting to give in. But Clara Lemlich and others knew that the right to unionize was critical to holding factory owners to their word. Without a union, the owners still had disproportionate power over working conditions. Owners could promise changes to working conditions and wages, but then take it all away on a moment's notice. If that happened, workers would be right back where they started. Unions were necessary to monitor labor policies in the long term.

Unfortunately, by February of 1910, the Triangle strikers simply couldn't hold out any longer. Blanck and Harris, along with other owners, refused to budge on the issue of unions. The owners were losing money while the strike was on, for sure, but they could go longer than the workers, who needed to eat and pay rent. It was February of 1910, and it was a cold winter. Workers couldn't afford heat, and they and their families were getting sick. So on February 15, 1909, after a twelve-week strike, the workers accepted a 12 percent wage increase (1 percent for each week of the strike) and a fifty-two-hour week, but they did so at the cost of a closed shop. That meant owners would not allow unions in the factories, and workers could be fired for joining a union. What the owners did agree to was to rehire strikers rather than firing them. (That didn't happen. Some strikers, particularly those who were identified as rabble-rousers, were fired.) Triangle also agreed to stop charging workers for the use of chairs, needles, and other work materials.

It was a win for workers, even if they didn't get everything they wanted. Perhaps even more important than the concessions they won (and those were quite important), the strike of 20,000 workers raised awareness. By 1910, just a year after the strike ended, 85 percent of New York garment workers were members of the ILGWU. Even in closed shops, owners had to admit that they were dealing with a union force that wasn't going to be stopped anytime soon.

That said, the fire at the Triangle Factory happened just a year later, so the deal fell far short of what the workers at the time really needed. Workers had been so focused on wages, hours, and union rights that they neglected safer working conditions. You didn't have to be a fire marshal to recognize hazardous conditions (like the presence of cigarettes in a room full of combustible materials). But owners simply had no incentive to improve the safety for their workers.

After the fire, Clara argued that the tragedy could have been prevented—or at least tempered—by the presence of a union that would have required basic safety standards, including requiring exit doors to be unlocked during working hours.

THE SHIRTWAIST KINGS FAILED THEIR WORKERS

No labor group, mink coats or not, could have been expected to fully reform such a powerful industry in just a few years. But they did what they could. Changes in working hours and wages represented gains in the labor movement, but that wasn't enough to protect the most vulnerable workers. Owners like Blanck and Harris were determined to maximize their gains and minimize their losses—and unfortunately they took little stock of human lives in their analysis. They could have saved the lives of everyone in the Asch Building with just a few small changes. That's a huge part of what makes the tragedy so heartbreaking. It seems inevitable now, but it didn't have to happen.

The Asch Building was a "fireproof" structure, which inspired a false sense of security among owners and occupants. Who could burn to death in a building made out of concrete and iron?

While it is true that the steel and concrete were fireproof, the owners had taken no precautions in case of a fire. There were not enough exits, not enough fire escapes in good repair, and not enough care taken to place fabrics and machines away from open flames. There were no fire drills, fire alarms, or rope ladders. The building withstood the fire, just as the builders promised, but anything inside of the building, including people, were ravaged.

After the fire, investigators would find many ways the tragedy could have been prevented, if only the owners had taken a few safety precautions. That discarded cigarette butt might not have become the catalyst for the worst workplace disaster in history at that time. The owners should have ensured that flammable materials were properly stored. They should have ensured that the standpipes were connected to functioning hoses. They should have had fire drills, fire escapes, overhead sprinklers, and fire ladders. They should have had unblocked exits. All those safety features were possible at the time, but they cost money—money that Blanck and Harris preferred to pocket rather than spend.

PREDATORY PRACTICES

Not just in the Triangle Factory but all over New York City, factory owners had figured out that fire safety was bad for the bottom line. Even if owners were willing to shell out a few bucks for sprinklers and escape ladders, the reality was that a safe building cost less to insure. You might be wondering why that's a bad thing. Wouldn't owners want lower insurance rates? That seems logical, but it wasn't the case in 1911. Insurance brokers preferred to insure unsafe buildings. The insurance rates for those buildings were much higher, which meant that insurance salesmen took a bigger cut on the insurance premium. And because the premiums were higher on unsafe buildings, the payouts to the owners, if there was a fire, were much higher.

In addition, factory owners knew that they could sometimes make money off a fire if they had a lot of extra stock. Here's how: If demand for shirtwaists was low, the factory might have a lot of extra material that owners had already paid for. If the materials went up in flames, the owners could claim that as a loss to the insurance company. That payout would often be more than they could've gotten if they'd actually produced garments. All of this meant that a fire could be a smart business move. That's not to say that all owners tried to start fires (although some certainly did)—or that they even wanted fires to happen. Put simply, some of the most successful owners worked within a system that rewarded harmful practices. A safety engineer by the name of E.F.J. Porter once reported hearing factory owners talk about how little the lives of their workers mattered to them. Porter said that one such owner said, in reference to workers, "Let 'em burn. They're a lot of cattle anyway."

Factory owners weren't the only people to blame for the Triangle fire. The New York City Building Department was supposed to regularly inspect the Triangle Factory, along with all the other factories in the city. After the fire, even the coroner—through his tears—accused the Building Department of being as guilty as anyone. The department responded by noting that it was low on funding and staff and therefore could not adequately inspect buildings unless they were newly constructed. Though regulations existed, the government provided no support to ensure regular and timely inspections.

A writer for a socialist newspaper at the time made the case that the real culprit was greed. As the writer put it: "These deaths resulted because capital begrudged the price of another fire escape." Trade union members draped a banner across Cooper Union with a plea: "We demand for all women the right to protect themselves." Even the fire chief spoke out, urging girls to refuse to work in factories where escape doors were locked. (Such a warning underscored the misguided belief that workers had the luxury to choose such a workplace.)

Isaac Harris and Max Blanck faced much public criticism, all of it well deserved. The Shirtwaist Kings were making money hand over fist by selling shirtwaists to wholesalers at a rate of about $18 per dozen. That comes out to about $1.50 per shirtwaist. Now remember that Blanck and Harris were paying their low-level workers around $3 per week. That meant that a worker cost the Kings just two shirtwaists a week. And workers produced far more than that. Anything above two shirtwaists a week was pure profit. You can see how the Kings were operating a gangbuster business, yet they were still obsessed with employee theft. That's why they insisted on keeping the factory doors locked. They were convinced that their employees, if given half a chance, would steal something. The Kings' preoccupation with theft cost dozens of girls their lives. Rabbi Stephen Wise, who led a memorial service on April 2, 1911, pointed out the tragedy of putting money above people:

> "The lesson of the hour is that while property is good, life is better, that while possessions are valuable, life is priceless. The meaning of the hour is that the life of the lowliest worker in the nation is sacred and inviolable, and, if that sacred human right be violated, we shall stand adjudged and condemned before the tribunal of God and of history."

Rabbi Wise's message was that people mattered more than profits. Even the lowest-rung worker deserved to be safe at work. Safety, Rabbi Wise and others argued, should be a human right, as inviolable as a person's right to life, liberty, and the pursuit of happiness.

AMERICA FINALLY PAYS ATTENTION

For those Americans who were lucky enough not to work in factories, the plight of the worker was fairly easy to ignore. Middle- and upper-class people had the luxury of walking past the hundreds of city factories every day without giving even a glancing thought to those who were stuck inside. All they knew was that any clothing they wanted could be purchased in brand-new department stores, emerging chain stores, and mail-order catalogs. Shopping was a new pastime for people with money. And they didn't have the opportunity or inclination to think about what human suffering went into the production of a pretty new shirtwaist. The labor strikes changed that. Americans of all social and economics classes had to sit up and take notice.

Many upper-class people labored under the illusion that young women were delicate beings who were easily led astray. For that reason, the prevailing belief was that women needed to stay at home while men went outside to work. The women would remain protected and unsullied by the grit of the world. The reality was that in 1910 almost a quarter of all women over the age of fifteen worked outside the home—often supporting entire families. And as we know, if they lived in the city and were white, they were probably working in factories. (People of color held jobs that were often far worse than factory jobs.) Seeing girls lining up on the strikes with their banners and picket signs, middle-class Americans had the opportunity to see women who were fighting their own fight, and clashing on equal terms with "men of the world." They were out there on the streets where anything might happen to them. That triggered paternalism in some people—a desire to protect these poor girls our all alone on the mean city streets. Make no mistake: This was a thoroughly sexist response. But it did win strikers some sympathy.

That sympathy was compounded when police—hired by the factory owners—started arresting picketers for disturbing the peace, loitering, or even prostitution (often without any evidence). In some cases, strikebreakers would hit a picketer, and then police would arrest the girl for assault! By December 1909, more than seven hundred workers had been arrested. Americans read the news reports with shock, surprised to see that the gritty reality of labor politics right before their eyes.

Not everyone felt sympathy for the strikers, however. Some people believed that women strikers deserved the treatment they were getting, and that they never should have left home in the first place. (Never mind that the factory workers weren't working for the fun of it.) Reporters at some of the more provocative papers didn't help matters when they started referring to the strikers as "socialists," "anarchists," or "agitators." As protesters were arrested and convicted of a variety of crimes (no matter how trumped up), it became hard for the general public to see them as sympathetic.

ROWS OF DEAD GIRLS

The Triangle fire changed that negative view of factory workers. When Americans picked up their newspapers on the morning after March 25, 1911, they saw a clear picture of victims, not criminals. They saw

A procession in honor of the victims of the fire.

dead girls lined up in a makeshift morgue. They saw bodies sprawled across the pavement. They read horror stories of girls who were faced with the choice of either jumping out of windows or being burned to death. It became much harder to blame the workers. Newspaper writers began to write more sympathetically about the workers. They used strong metaphors in their phototext (the words they wrote to caption photographs) that presented the Asch Building as "a death trap" and the workers as "products" or "consumer goods" that the owners exploited. Those metaphors gave readers "new understandings of and actions toward justice" and encouraged them to take action against factory owners.

Newspapers used illustrations to get readers' attention as well. On March 27, the *New York World* ran an editorial cartoon featuring an image of Death inside the Asch Building. He's holding an unfurled scroll that says, "New York Factory Regulations," and under that is Death's signature with an "ok." That same day, the *New York Evening Journal* ran a cartoon of a girl lying dead on the pavement below the Asch Building. The caption says, "This Is One of a Hundred Murdered. Is any one to be punished for this?"

After the Triangle fire, America was ready to pay attention to the immigrant workers who had suffered for so long. Finally, America was ready for change.

CHAPTER 10

AFTER THE FLAMES

I turned the knob this way and that. I pushed it toward myself and I couldn't open it; then I pushed it inward and it wouldn't go...I knocked at the door. I seen [sic] the flames were too strong...I stood at that door still till the last minute.

—Katie Weiner

I tried to turn the handle and it would not bend. It was locked.

—Lillian Weiner

Let's go back to that horrible afternoon of March 25, 1911. After just eighteen minutes, 144 people were dead. (Two more would die of their injuries later.) Fortunately, 350-some people made it out alive. They were simply lucky. That's all it came down to in the end: Some were lucky, and some were not.

Remember the five Triangle girls we met in the first chapter? Let's see what happened to them.

ANNIE MILLER (16), THE FIGHTER

Annie was the brave girl who ran back into the factory to save her friends. Last we saw, she'd hustled them onto the last elevator going down, but before she could board the elevator car, she fell. Other girls desperate to get to the elevator trampled over her. By the time she was able to get up, injured by the trampling, she knew the elevator wouldn't be returning. She made a split-second decision and hobbled toward the windows. That decision was the perhaps the worst one she could have made, but she was out of options. The windows were all she had left.

Annie found herself standing at the large windows with the fire raging behind her. There was no way she could run for the stairs, not without walking into the flames. The smoke was rising, making it difficult to breathe. She was in the midst of the fire at its absolute peak, and she'd lost her opportunity to make it to an unobstructed exit when she attempted to help her coworkers.

She had seconds to decide what to do before her lungs filled with smoke. So she did the only thing she could do: She jumped.

By all rights, the jump should have killed her. By some miracle, she didn't die on impact. She was breathing, but she was unconscious. She was rushed to St. Vincent's Hospital, where she remained in a coma for several days. She had a fractured leg and many internal injuries, but she was awake and talking after a few days. It seemed she was going to survive. She wasn't just a heroine for saving her friends; she was a miracle case who survived injuries that by all rights should have killed her. Fifty-eight people died from jumping out the windows that day.

It seemed that fate was on Annie's side, that she would pull through and go on to live a happy life—but then the unthinkable happened. After what seemed to be a miraculous recovery, Annie lost consciousness on April 5, 1911. She died that same day. She had survived more than a week with injuries far more serious than anyone realized, but her strength wasn't enough to save her.

Annie Miller—the heroine, the fighter, the girl who seemed to beat the odds—lost the battle. The Triangle fire took her life.

BESSIE GABRILOWICH (19), THE BIG SISTER

Bessie was the girl who was so worried about her friend Dora, whom she'd sent to ask the boss for a raise just before the fire broke out. Dora didn't make it out of the building alive that day. Bessie probably didn't know that when she ran. All she knew was that everyone who was left needed to get out and get out fast. With her purse covering her face to make breathing easier, she took off down the stairs as the flames chased her.

Bessie survived that day because she ran to the stairs instead of the windows or the elevators, as many of the other girls did. She was lucky in that she was closest to the stairwell with unlocked doors. Those girls who lined up at the locked exits were simply not as fortunate.

A day or so after the fire, Bessie returned to the Asch Building. When she saw the rows of bodies lined up on the sidewalk, she collapsed. At that moment, a reporter took her photo. Bessie kept that photo all her life, a grim reminder of what she had survived.

Years later, Bessie still vividly remembered the horror of that day. She never wanted to forget, despite the pain it must have caused her. She knew that her duty to her lost colleagues and her friend Dora was to ensure that nobody ever stopped thinking about those girls.

Happily, Bessie did live a full life. She worked other factory jobs after the fire and joined the International Ladies' Garment Workers' Union to fight for workers' rights. Four years after the fire, in 1915, she married Lewis Cohen. They moved to Connecticut and had two children, a son, Jack, and a daughter, Sylvia. She and Cohen divorced after twenty-five years of marriage, and Bessie moved to Los Angeles to be closer to Jack.

All her life, Bessie was a courageous and independent woman. When she was eighty-nine, she was mugged in the street by two men who stole her purse and broke her jaw. But that didn't slow Bessie down. Even though she had to eat through a straw while her jaw was wired shut, she went back home to her working-class Boyle Heights neighborhood, determined not to let the unsavory criminals chase her out.

When she was ninety-three, she moved to a nursing home. Before she left for the care facility, two hundred of her neighbors threw her a going-away party. The nursing home ended up being Bessie's home for fourteen years. She no doubt made two hundred new friends there.

Bessie lived to be a whopping 107 years old. She died in 1999, one of the very last Triangle survivors who were still around. Through all the years she drew breath, the girls of Triangle survived in Bessie's heart.

ROSE ROSENFELD (17), THE THINKER

Last we saw Rose, she was in the middle of the fire on the ninth floor. Rose wasn't one to panic, so when she cleared her head to think, she came up with a question, one that ultimately saved her life: What are the executives doing? That was exactly the right question to be asking, because the answer led her to the tenth floor.

She climbed up the smoky stairs while everyone else on her floor was running down them. She choked on the smoke as she went up. She had no idea what she was going to find. For all she knew, that floor might turn out to be a wall of fire as well, and she'd be trapped.

Rose soon saw that the tenth floor was smoky too, but there was a way out. She discovered what the tenth-floor workers and bosses, including owners Harris and Blanck, had already figured out: The stairway was open to the roof, and the window offered an escape path to the NYU building next door. As the *New York Times* noted much later, Rose was one of just a few people who managed to be clearheaded in the time of a crisis. That rational thinking saved her life. She made a snap decision, and it turned out to be the right one.

Once she was on the tenth floor, the improvised rescue squad on the other side saw her and helped her climb across the ladder to the NYU building. Once safely across, she walked down the stairs and exited out onto the street. Only then did she see the bodies falling from the ninth-floor windows.

Days later, Harris and Blanck found a new location for the factory and resumed business. Rose could have returned to her job, but she didn't. She simply couldn't face it. Instead, Rose used her savings to go to college. She eventually married a man named Harry Freedman, an American whom she met in Vienna. They had three children. When Harry died in 1959, Rose went back to work, supporting her three children by herself. Rose's task was made even harder by the fact that two of her children had polio. She worked in a Manhattan insurance company until she was close to eighty years old, lying about her age to keep from being forced into retirement.

When Rose was seventy-nine, she decided it was time to retire.

Little did she know that she would live for twenty-eight more years! In those years, she made good use of her time. She learned to paint, and to speak new languages. (She was 107 when she began learning her seventh language—Spanish.) And she was a die-hard Los Angeles Lakers fan until her dying day.

Rose remained a tireless supporter of workers and labor rights her entire life. While it was difficult for her to talk about what happened that day, she told her story often because, like other survivors, she didn't want those who had died to be forgotten. The victims paid with their lives because Blanck and Harris, and other owners like them, wanted to make tons of money. Rose never stopped telling the world that the welfare of workers mattered then, just as it matters now.

Rose died in 2001. Before she died, she told a filmmaker what she thought about the fire:

That's the whole trouble of this fire. Nobody cares. Nobody. Hundred forty-six people in a half an hour. I have always tears in my eyes when I think. It should never have happened. The executives with a couple of steps could have opened the door. But they thought they were better than the working people. It's not fair because material, money, is more important here than everything. That's the biggest mistake—that a person doesn't count much when he hasn't got money. What good is a rich man and he hasn't got a heart? I don't pretend. I feel it. Still.

FANNIE LANSNER (21), THE LEADER

Fannie was used to leading the other girls. That was her job, after all. She was responsible for making sure everyone completed their work on time and with minimal errors. When the fire broke out, Fannie did what came naturally to her: She calmly led the others to safety. When we saw her last, she was standing outside the elevator. The doors had closed and the car was descending. Fannie waited, but the elevator wasn't coming back. She had to make a choice. Should she jump down the elevator shaft? Should she fight the smoke and flames and try to get across the room to the stairway? Or should she follow the others who were going to the windows?

In the end, Fannie ran for the windows. On that day, she was among the fifty-eight people who died after jumping. She saw no other choice, no other way out, and so she stepped up to the window ledge and took the leap.

Fannie undoubtedly saved many lives by guiding people to the elevator and helping them line up to get in the elevator car. Her patience and calm demeanor were a miracle amid the chaos, and she sacrificed her life for her girls. The *New York Evening Telegram* ran a headline that proclaimed Fannie's courage while underscoring the depth of her sacrifice: "Heroic Young Forewomen Loses Her Life from Death in Flames: Guides Girls To Safety Until Her Own Escape Cut Off... THEN LEAPS FROM WINDOW TO DEATH ON PAVEMENT."

A hundred and some years after her death, Fannie's great-nephew imagined in a newspaper article how his great-aunt would feel about labor policies and attitudes toward workers today. He concluded that she "would empathize with the plight of today's overworked, underemployed and lightly compensated worker." Based on what we know about Fannie, we would say he's exactly right.

KATE LEONE (14), THE BABY

Kate was one of the youngest workers at the Triangle Factory that Saturday afternoon. Last we saw little Kate, she was in the middle of a swarm of girls moving from a locked door to the elevator. She was fighting to stay on her feet. If she fell, she would have been trampled by the crowd.

Recall that Kate had only been on the job for a few weeks, but her cousins had been there longer. She was trying to find them in the crowd, but there were too many people running in every direction, and the smoke was so thick. It must have been hard to see anything.

Kate's cousins, Annie Colletti and Michelina Nicolosei, didn't make it out alive. Kate's uncle, Dominick Leone, went to the morgue and identified the bodies of Annie and Michelina shortly after the fire. But there was no sign of Kate there. Devastated, Kate's family waited for news of their baby.

On March 27, two days after the fire, Dominick saw a shoe on a body that appeared to be Kate's. He knelt closer to the body and used a small knife to cut a lock of hair close to her head where the flames hadn't reached her. He showed that lock of hair to one of Kate's sisters. The sister cried in anguish. This was their Kate. This charred body was their precious sister, daughter, niece. Everyone in the family sobbed for their loss.

Medical personnel later concluded that Kate collapsed not far from the elevators and died of smoke inhalation. She was one of forty-nine others who died from suffocation or burns and was one of the very last people to be identified.

Just two years after Kate's death, her parents had another baby. They named her Kate—in honor of her big sister.

WHO SHOULD PAY FOR THIS TRAGEDY?

It's hard to read these stories and not be affected by the tragedies and the sorrows of so many people. Even the survivors have bittersweet stories. They lived, but they were haunted by the memories of all those innocent people who died.

After the fire, people demanded justice. The survivors, their families, the families of the victims, union supporters, and even some politicians wanted to see the Triangle owners, Harris and Blanck, punished for how little they seemed to care for the lives of their employees.

ON TRIAL

After looking at all the information that had come to light since the fire, a grand jury issued an indictment. Isaac Harris and Max Blanck were charged with manslaughter. Max D. Steuer represented Harris and Blanck, while Assistant District Attorneys Robert Rubin and Charles S. Bostwick represented the people. On December 4, 1911, the trial began with jury selection. It was a cold, windy day in New York, and the city was covered with five inches of fresh snow. It was so cold in the courtroom that Harris and Blanck wore their overcoats for a good part of the day. When Blanck finally took his coat off, he revealed

Max Blanck and Isaac Harris

a diamond pin tucked into the lapel of his suit. His outfit was in sharp contrast to those worn by the observers who filled the courtroom—mostly working-class family members and friends of the fire victims dressed in mourning clothes.

On the following day, December 5, the selected jury members took their seats to listen to evidence from both sides. Supporters of the Triangle victims mobbed Blanck and Harris as they exited the courthouse elevator. The crowd yelled, "Murderers! Murderers! Make them suffer for killing our children." Some people waved photos of their dead children and shouted, "These are our children! Give us back our children!" The cries rang out in English and Yiddish alike.

Harris and Blanck shrank back. Their attorney, however, was not intimidated. Max Steuer was only five feet tall, but he pushed his way through the crowd, leading his clients to the courtroom. Police came several minutes later and cleared the hallway. At the lunch break, the crowds were back, following Harris and Blanck and jeering at them.

The trial lasted for eighteen days. Over the course of the trial, the prosecution and the defense called a total of 150 witnesses to the stand. The attorneys on both sides addressed a number of issues, but the trial hinged around one central question: whether or not the factory doors were locked. The prosecution called Triangle survivors to the stand to testify that they tried the doors and couldn't open them. The defense in turn called several witnesses who claimed either that the doors were unlocked or that there was a key hanging near each door (meaning that even if the door was locked, anyone could have opened it). Steuer also argued that the girls didn't use the exit because the stairwell was consumed with fire. That argument was specious because those who exited from the unlocked tenth-floor door were able to descend those very same stairs without being engulfed in flames. Steuer argued that the girls who said the doors were locked—or that they didn't see flames in the stairwells—were lying because they had lost friends and were overcome with grief.

Bostwick and Rubin, representing the people, argued that Harris and Blanck showed a callous disregard for the safety and well being of their employees. Steuer unwittingly helped with that argument when Harris got on the stand and argued that employee theft was a constant threat to his profits. Yet when questioned further, he admitted that losses from theft had amounted to no more than $25 in total, a statement that Steuer most certainly wished Harris hadn't admitted because it made him look petty. While $25 was a lot of money to a working-class person, it certainly wasn't for Harris and Blanck. Triangle was the largest shop in the business, producing mass quantities of shirtwaists. A dozen of these sold wholesale for between $16 and $18. For all of the anxiety Harris expressed about stolen goods, he admitted that he and his partner lost no more than a dozen and a half shirtwaists to theft. Total. This isn't to say that theft is ever right, but it showed the jury that Harris and Blanck were deeply mistrustful of their employees without good reason. It also showed that they had little respect or regard for their workers in general. Ethel Monick, a Triangle worker, took the stand and drove that point home: "But, you know, I was like nothing to them because I was only a working girl."

Bostwick and Rubin's witnesses swore that the doors were locked, citing as evidence that the doors were always locked due to Blanck and Harris's obsessive fear of theft. Bostwick even brought to the court-room a velvet-lined wooden box (like the kind you might use to keep good silverware) and dramatically opened it for the jury. Inside the box was a lock still attached to a wooden piece of a door. The piece had been recovered by firefighters. Bostwick revealed that this lock was from the ninth-floor door, and the display proved that the door was locked at the time of the fire.

Steuer came back with a barrage of arguments that didn't always cohere: that the door was unlocked, that the door was locked but that a key was always hanging nearby on a piece of a string, that the girls didn't try the door before running to the windows, that theft was so common that the owners were forced to lock doors and search employees and therefore were quite justified. The list goes on. It's hard to figure out how these arguments fit together. If the witnesses said the door was unlocked, why the arguments about the key? If theft was so rampant and required constant vigilance, why the argument that the door was unlocked and was always unlocked?

The convoluted defense arguments suggested to some that the defense was doing anything it could to elude responsibility, an idea that the prosecution tried hard to make stick with jurors. When both sides were through presenting their arguments, the jury left the courtroom and began deliberation at 2:55 p.m. on December 27, 1911. Before they left, the judge urged them to think carefully about the evidence presented. Their job, he said, was to focus on whether or not evidence existed that the doors were locked and whether or not the prosecution had sufficiently proven Harris and Blanck knew that the doors were locked. Less than two hours later, the jury returned with their answer.

Not guilty.

ENOUGH BLAME TO GO AROUND

Not surprisingly, Harris and Blanck were relieved by the verdict. The friends and families of the victims, however, were outraged. Some of the jurors later explained their reasoning. One said that he believed the door was locked, but the prosecution could not prove that Harris and Blanck knew it was locked. Perhaps someone else had locked the doors? How could the jurors know? Reluctantly, he had to vote not guilty. If state inspectors had been on trial, he added, he would have voted for their conviction. (More about the state inspectors in a bit.) Another juror said he voted not guilty because nobody was at fault. It was an act of God, he maintained.

The public was outraged by the verdict. In their minds, Harris and Blanck had gotten away with murder, quite literally. And they knew that the public hated them. Immediately after the fire, before the trial even began, Harris and Blanck shelled out almost $5,000 in advertising for the Triangle Factory. It did little to improve public perception. The scheme backfired and made them look manipulative at best.

Harris and Blanck had a poor track record when it came to fire and fire safety since even before the 1911 fire. Between 1902 and 1910, a whopping eight different fires led to employee injuries. Five of the fires happened at the Triangle Factory. Two happened at the Diamond Waist Company, their other shop. And one happened at Harris's home. Two of the Triangle Factory incidents were small fires started by cigarettes and were quickly extinguished. Those two fires, in 1908 and 1909, did suggest that cigarette fires were a problem that Harris and Blanck were aware of. The other fires occurred late at night or early in the morning and resulted in huge insurance payouts. We know for sure that Harris and Blanck collected at least $32,000 in insurance payments for two of those fires. The other four late-night or early-morning fires resulted in payouts as well, but we don't know how much. We can guess that those payouts were similar to the first two, and we can safely estimate that they collected $60,000 or more in insurance money between 1902 and 1907. Today, that would be the equivalent to over a million dollars.

We have no proof that Harris and Blanck started those fires themselves. We do know, however, that fires were often a windfall for factory owners. Insurance fraud was rampant. Insurance salesmen and brokers made a ton of money on high premiums paid for by factories with few safety features (like overhead sprinklers, for instance). Factories were willing to pay those high premiums because the payouts—if there was a fire—were big.

Some experts estimate that if Harris and Blanck had upgraded the Triangle's safety features—and paid lower premiums—the salesmen and brokers would have made $2 million less per year. It's no wonder that they didn't install sprinklers or other safety features. It didn't make financial sense to them or to their insurance brokers. So even though the Triangle was known as a "rotten risk" in the insurance industry, nobody cared.

Harris and Blanck collected almost $65,000 in insurance money as a result of the 1911 fire. Put it this way: They made $445 per casualty. Harris and Blanck actually made money at the cost of their workers' lives. They didn't cause the fire directly, and they didn't want all those girls to die, but the decisions they made allowed them to maximize profits without considering the human cost.

EVERYONE IS CULPABLE

Harris and Blanck were not the only people who made bad decisions prior to the Triangle fire of 1911. City officials could have (and should have) shouldered some of the blame. Those city officials were responsible for inspecting building plans for proper safety features, but they didn't do the job properly. Public officials, with almost no exceptions, were appalled by the fire, but none wanted to take responsibility. In the months after the fire, city officials played the blame game, looking to push responsibility to whomever was closest. For instance, when inspectors came to evaluate the fire damage, they noted the almost useless fire escape. Each city official claimed that another, different department was the one who was responsible for ensuring that the fire escape was functional.

At the trial, the jury learned that the Asch Building actually did meet many of the standards of city regulations. The problem was that the regulations were flawed. For example, New York required each worker to have 250 cubic feet in the workplace. That's about the size of a closet. It's not a huge amount of space, but it does ensure that workers aren't pushed together elbow to elbow. Factory owners, however, hit upon a brilliant solution (brilliant for them, not for workers) to subvert the required space regulation. Construction companies built the new factory spaces in New York with extremely high ceilings. So employees in newer buildings—like the Asch Building—could actually have less space on the floor than they had before. All the government-required space was above their heads, which did the workers no good when they were crammed together at sewing tables. And it certainly did not do them any good when they were rushing out of a building that didn't have a functioning fire escape, or that had three fewer staircases than were required by law.

The Asch Building represented a particular problem for city officials when it came to regulations of any kind. That's because different people disagreed about whether or not the initial plans, submitted in 1900, had been approved. Some reports said that the Triangle Factory was never in compliance, all the way back to 1902 when Harris and

Coroner Holzhauser investigates the roof of the Asch Building along with Assistant District Attorneys J. Robert Rubin and Charles Bostwick.

Blanck operated on the ninth floor only. Other reports claimed that as the Triangle Factory grew, taking over the eighth floor in 1906 and the tenth floor in 1908, the conditions became unsafe. And city officials argued that because of the explosion of new buildings in New York, it was simply impossible to inspect them on a regular basis. So even if the Asch Building would have failed an inspection in 1911, it probably wouldn't have mattered, because no one was there to enforce that judgment.

The general public had no idea that factory conditions inside the building had gotten so bad. After the Triangle fire, newspaper writers, politicians, and labor union supporters made it their mission to make sure everyone knew all the ways that factory owners across the city were creatively eluding the law, and that city officials were shirking their duties.

From the day after the fire until after the trial, people spoke out about the tragedy and decried the lack of safety for American workers. The coroner who was called on-site after the fire saw the rickety fire escape and was reduced to tears. He remembered saying, "Only one little fire escape! I shall proceed against the Building Department along with the others. They are as guilty as any. They haven't been insistent enough and these poor girls who were carried up in the elevator to work in the morning came down in the evening at the end of a fireman's rope."

Lillian D. Wald of the Joint Board of Sanitary Control was equally outraged. She contributed to a report about the Asch Building conditions. She wrote, in part, "The conditions as they now exist are hideous and damnable. Our investigators have shown that there are hundreds of buildings which invite disaster just as much as did the Asch structure. The crux of the situation is that there is no direct responsibility. Divided, always divided! The responsibility rests nowhere!"

The public wanted someone to blame. Corrupt government officials and ruthless factory owners, who for so long had been above the law, were a natural target. Rabbi Wise called out greed in no uncertain terms: "If we have no money for the necessary enforcement of the laws which safeguard the lives of workers it is because of so much of our money is wasted and squandered and stolen."

PROGRESSIVISM TAKES ROOT

With so many young girls dead as a direct result of mismanagement and boundless greed, it was hard for the public to find any silver lining. But the Triangle fire did give rise to some very positive changes. It represented a turning point, a change in public sentiment, a new perspective on the perils of the American Dream when left unchecked. Nothing changed overnight, but the Triangle fire convinced many people that workers deserved to be safe in the workplace. The idea that workplace safety might be a human right is so engrained in our minds now that it's hard to believe that there was a time, fairly recently in fact, when we didn't think that way. We owe our workplace safety today to the victims of the Triangle fire and those who fought tirelessly to change the laws.

After the fire, the Women's Trade Union League (WTUL) began surveying factory workers. They asked factory girls to fill out a questionnaire that had questions like, "In your shop or factory, are the doors locked? Are there any bars on the windows? Are the freight elevator doors closed during the day? Are there fire escapes on all floors and is there free access to the fire escapes? Are there any scraps near the motor or engine?"

The WTUL and other unions were part of a greater social movement called progressivism. Progressives had three main goals. The first was to stop authorities' abuse of power. The second was for Americans to identify as a collective group with similar interests rather than competing individuals competing against each other for scarce resources. Finally, progressives believed in data. They wanted to study everything and then use technical experts to fix broken systems. Progressivism was a celebration of pragmatism and science.

REDEFINING GOVERNMENT

Progressives also wanted to change how we as a country defined freedom, especially as it related to the role of government. Factory owners, the people who were getting rich from exploitative labor practices, seemed to think that freedom meant being able to do whatever they wanted, even if that resulted in hurting other people. Progressives believed extreme individualism should not infringe on the common good. If it did, as we saw in this era, no American was truly free. Everyone was then at the mercy of an unequal system.

For that reason, progressives asserted that government must research problems in the system; use science and expertise to identify solutions; and then solve those problems, even if that meant passing laws to restrict trade or commerce somewhat. The progressives believed this philosophy was in keeping with the spirit of the Founding Fathers, men who were afraid of unrestrained power of any kind, whether it came from the government or from capitalist industries. We must protect ourselves from ourselves, according to progressive ideals.

Progressives believed that the Triangle fire was a tragic catalyst, an event that could teach us much about what needed to change inside not just the Triangle Factory (which continued production after the fire) but in factories at large. The progressive movement was in full swing prior to 1911, but for the first time, progressives had America's full attention. In the three years after the fire, the United States passed thirty-six different laws designed to protect workers, many of which still exist today.

TRUST BUSTERS

Progressives had long wanted to right the wrongs of the Gilded Age. Remember that the late 1800s and early 1900s was an era in which a select few people accrued unprecedented wealth, often at the expense of immigrant women and children. Progressives studied the issue of worker exploitation across the United States and determined one very important cause of the problem: trusts.

Trusts are large companies that attempt to gain control of a market by buying up smaller competing companies and/or supplier companies. With all lines of supply owned by the same person, he could set prices and control the market.

Here's another way of thinking about trusts: Suppose you own a company that makes widgets. As your widget company grows, you can afford to sell your widgets at a lower price than your competitors. Eventually, you'll put other sellers out of business who can't compete with your pricing. Then you start buying up all those smaller widget sellers. Soon you have so much money that you even start buying the companies that supply the materials to manufacture the widgets. Before long, you are the only widget seller, and you control every aspect of widget production. You can now raise the price of your widgets, and customers will be forced to buy your product because no other widget manufacturer exists. And nobody else can get in the game because you own and control all the supplies. You now have a widget monopoly.

In the early 1900s, you wouldn't have been required to pay any federal income taxes either. On top of that, you would have had minimal safety requirements to follow, so you wouldn't have to worry about spending money on fire alarms or fire escapes in your manufacturing factories. (It was a pretty sweet time to be a trust, admittedly.)

As this example shows, your widget manufacturing company would have been a raging success…for you at least. And if you ever felt guilty about the people who worked for you, you could tell yourself that it was just the natural order of things.

THE MEATPACKING INDUSTRY

One of the biggest trusts in the early 1900s was the meatpacking industry. Just six companies controlled the entire market, and together they formed the National Packing Company, making $700 million a year. (That's about $20 billion in today's dollars.) Competition was utterly impossible. Consumers were at the mercy of whatever prices were set by the owners, and workers were forced to labor under terrible conditions because they had nowhere else to go. Injuries on the job were common. Many people died because the meatpacking factories were so unsafe.

In 1905 the U.S. Supreme Court ruled against the National Packing Company for being in violation of the Sherman Antitrust Act, an 1890 law that prohibited multiple business from acting together to create a monopoly and control prices. The act was a big victory for the American people, but there was still much work to be done when it came to trusts in other industries.

THE FOUR HUNDRED

Trusts gave rise to handful of ultra-wealthy people. These people were nicknamed the "Four Hundred," a reference to the number of people that could comfortably fit in the Astor family's ballroom. Mrs. Astor notably remarked upon building the Astor home that the ballroom needn't accommodate more than four hundred people since only four hundred people in the country were worth inviting anyway. Mrs. Astor wasn't terribly far off. In 1900, 1 percent of the entire population held 99 percent of the wealth. That's hardly surprising given that 305 trusts existed in 1904. They controlled almost 100 percent of manufacturing in the entire country.

Not all of these people were motivated by simple money lust, however. Andrew Carnegie, the extraordinarily wealthy steel magnate, gave away tons of money. He made roughly $10 million a year, an extraordinary sum when the national average was just $500 a year. But Carnegie gave away more than $300 million of his fortune over the course of the early 1900s.

Carnegie was born poor in 1835 in Scotland. He moved to Pennsylvania with his parents in the 1840s. Carnegie, just a child, immediately went to work as a bobbin boy in a cotton mill. Bobbin boys brought the girls a bobbin, a small spindle for winding yarn or thread, as the girls called for them. Carnegie was a hard worker and quickly found a better position as a telegraph boy. He paid close attention to how telegraphs operated and eventually moved up to being an operator. Unlike many immigrants, he was able to save his money rather than having to simply send it off to family members in another country. With money borrowed from a successful friend, he bought shares in the Adams Express Company. It wasn't long before he had the capital to invest in the industry that made him unimaginably wealthy: the steel industry.

While Carnegie was certainly generous with his wealth, he still earned much of his money on the backs of his employees. His steel workers put in long hours for low wages, and they constantly feared they would lose their jobs. Under those conditions, Carnegie increased productivity by 800 percent.

Like many titans of industry, Carnegie eschewed governmental regulation of the markets. Yet as a business owner he benefited from governmental support and subsidies. Though Carnegie was generous in many ways, he simply didn't understand the lives of his workers. Yes, Carnegie worked very hard for his wealth, but he didn't acquire it by hard work alone. He borrowed capital, which was the key to success in America at the time (and that may still be true now). Most titans of industry had help from family members or were lucky enough to have contacts who could fund their start-ups, facts that they often conveniently forgot about when they presented themselves as self-made men. They often supported regulation for others, but not themselves. Carnegie and the Rockefellers, for instance, were very much against speculation, yet both families benefited from speculation.

Even if trust holders were generous with their wealth—and many were—they still built a system that was inarguably exploitative of workers. That's why the progressives took on trusts and made it their mission to bust them, to end the business practices that benefited a handful and exploited millions. One of the most famous trust busters was Theodore Roosevelt, president of the United States from 1901 to 1909. Trust busting became his mission, but not because he didn't believe in big business or big profits. Roosevelt was an unapologetic capitalist. But he also believed that business had to be responsible. They had to consider how their practices impacted the American worker and the markets at large.

Here's how Roosevelt put it after he determined not to run for another term in office (no laws existed at the time preventing someone from being elected for more than two terms):

> "There was crusading to do when I took hold. There was something that had to be uprooted…The conscience of business had to be aroused, the authority of the government over big as well as small had to be asserted."

TAMING BIG BUSINESS

Roosevelt took on many of the biggest trusts when he was in office. Under his watch, forty-four monopolies dissolved. He also regulated the railroads, meaning that he protected consumers against monopolies and unreasonable prices. He signed the Meat Inspection Act and the Pure Food and Drug Act, both of which regulated food production and protected the health of American consumers. It's no surprise that Roosevelt is considered a hero of the progressive movement, a shining example of the good things that can happen when government uses its power to protect people rather than turn a blind eye to corruption.

Roosevelt wasn't alone in his beliefs. Progressives were everywhere, even in New York where Tammany Hall had a longstanding alliance with big businesses, whether they harmed people or not. But by 1910 Tammany Hall had a new leader by the name of Alfred E. Smith, a man who believed, like Roosevelt, that the government had an obligation to enforce workplace safety. Smith argued that Tammany Hall should be proactive and work to prevent accidents, rather than just pitching in after they occurred. Smith vowed that another tragedy like the Triangle fire would not happen again. He led a factory inspection commission that sought to learn what was really going on behind closed (and locked) doors. That commission led to thirty new laws, all designed to protect workers.

Woodrow Wilson, elected president in 1912, followed suit with his own progressive agenda. He pushed for changes in legislation and regulation that would allow small corporations to compete with bigger ones. He signed the Clayton Antitrust Act, passed by Congress in 1912, which added further protections for small businesses. The act outlawed price fixing and other unfair business practices that had allowed trusts to flourish in the Gilded Age and beyond. Wilson recognized that if just a few men controlled most of American industry, they had the power to throw the entire country into a financial panic. The Clayton Antitrust Act was designed to protect the American people from being controlled by a few corporations. Wilson also backed the Sixteenth Amendment, which established a national income tax, and supported the Federal Trade Commission and the Federal Reserve, both of which were designed to ensure that the government could protect people from corporate greed and bad or unsafe business practices.

Perhaps the most important achievement of the progressive era was the passing of legislation that directly protected the most vulnerable workers: immigrants and unskilled workers. By 1912, thirty-eight states banned child labor. In 1916 Wilson signed into law the Keating-Owen Child Labor Act, which outlawed child labor. According to the law, you had to be at least sixteen years old to be lawfully employed. It is a law that we still recognize today in most industries. Not only did that law protect children in factories, but it protected those children who were exploited in rural areas as well. In 1914 a reporter by the name of Lewis Hine reported a story on kids who worked on farms. He found a four-year-old who picked ten pounds of cotton a day. Her five-year-old sister picked thirty pounds a day. Hine discovered that many farmworkers who did backbreaking labor (most of them black children) were unprotected by any laws forbidding exploitation.

Outlawing child labor did more than protect children from unsafe and exploitative working situations. Wilson recognized that child labor forced wages down for everyone. If a farm owner or a factory owner could pay a child just pennies for her work, he had no incentive to hire an adult for more money.

One of Wilson's crowning achievements is another law still in place today. That's the law mandating an eight-hour workday. Prior to that law, employers could force workers to work as many hours as they demanded. Keep in mind that most people weren't paid hourly, so employers quickly figured out that requiring more hours of employees yielded more output for less money. Wilson's law prohibited owners from requiring more than eight-hour days without compensation. If an employee worked nine hours, she was entitled to overtime pay.

CONSUMER PROTECTION

The progressive agenda focused on more than just protecting workers. Progressives also wanted to protect consumers. Since every American was a consumer—some certainly more than others—the consumer protection laws that grew out of the early 1900s were good for everybody. These are laws that still protect us today.

Prior to the early 1900s, almost no consumer protection laws existed. That's partially because we didn't need them. Before the rise of factory production and big department stores, buyers and sellers knew each other. If you bought medicine from your family doctor and it made you sick, you knew exactly where to go to complain about that product. And because your family doctor depended on you to make a living, he had an incentive to ensure that his products were pure and safe.

But as the world got bigger and industry expanded, people didn't necessarily know who made the products they bought and consumed. Magazine writers started researching and publishing exposés on quack medicine, like Lydia Pinkham's Vegetable Compound, a tincture that claimed to cure any "female complaint." Ladies who suffered from any ache or pain were encouraged to write to Mrs. Pinkham for advice. They'd receive a letter back, one suggesting that they buy Lydia Pinkham's Vegetable Compound. According to advertising copy, it was:

> "A sure cure for PROLAPSUS UTERI, or falling of the womb and all FEMALE WEAKNESSES including leucorrhoea, irregular and painful menstruation, inflammation and ulceration of the womb, flooding...for all weaknesses of the generative organs of either sex, it is second to no remedy that has ever been before the public, and for all diseases of the kidneys it is the GREATEST REMEDY IN THE WORLD."

Investigative journalists later revealed that Mrs. Pinkham did not exist; instead, inquiries were answered by a team of hired typists who simply copied a form letter. When the Pure Food and Drug Act was passed, the makers of Mrs. Pinkham's tincture were required to reveal the content of the so-called wonder medicine. Any guesses to the main ingredient? If you guessed alcohol, you are right. The compound was up to 20 percent alcohol. No wonder it cured everything!

The progressives did improve American life and culture through regulations, laws, and education. Americans of all kinds soon began to recognize that everyone deserved to be safe in their homes and workplaces. Though life certainly improved for many people after the Triangle fire, some were not so lucky. Factory workers did slowly win more rights, including the right to unionize, and most were safer at work than in the past, but not everyone was treated with respect and dignity.

BLACK GIRLS AND LATINAS IN AMERICA

You might have noticed by now that the factory girls we've met have all been white. That's because women of color, particularly black women, were simply not hired at factories. Racism was so pervasive that even the worst jobs—jobs that were criminally underpaid, backbreaking, and dangerous to personal health—were awarded to white women over black women.

When labor organizations began leading strikes, factory owners opened the door to black girls and women to take those jobs vacated by whites. Black women would have had every right to take the jobs; after all, many were being paid peanuts to do domestic jobs, if they were lucky enough to even have a job. Those black women who did work in factories were excluded from joining the American Federation of Labor (AFL), one of the most important labor organizations. The AFL claimed that it didn't ban black members, but it would do things like charge high fees or forbid memberships to anyone without an apprenticeship. Those barriers to entry effectively banned black women, even if that wasn't the AFL's stated policy. Many black women refused to accept those factory jobs during labor strikes, not because the labor unions had done anything for them, but because they knew that everyone had to stand together, even if the culture was openly racist.

Beginning in 1901, over one million black people headed north to work in factories. Before that, most black Americans lived in the rural South. Life outside the city wasn't much better than life in it. In Little Rock, Arkansas, a laundry owner explained why he could pay black women less than white women: "Because they can live in a little old shack house and they don't care what they eat, anyhow." Sadly, that notion that black people were somehow less human than white people, and that they were therefore entitled to less, was not uncommon. Those laundry workers that the owner so cruelly dismissed worked six days a week in a room that was 115 degrees.

Organizing in any way was rare, especially given that prior to 1900, 45 percent of all black people in America couldn't read. Even ten years later, after progressive changes made education more accessible, illiteracy for the black population was still at 30 percent. And in many areas of the American South, voting laws required literacy (and that was no coincidence). When black people would attempt to enroll in schools in order to learn to read—and thus register to vote—they would be turned away. It was legal for many years to deny access to public education. (And even when it was illegal, people did it anyway.) It wasn't until 1910 when Booker T. Washington formed the National Association for the Advancement of Colored People (NAACP), an organization that advocated for black people who were victimized and marginalized by a culture that privileged whites.

And of course it wasn't just black women who were subject to racism. In Tampa, Florida, Cuban women kept the cigar industry afloat. They made cigars—a task that's dirty and labor intensive—for hours a day, only to make a few pennies. Their labor is how cigar makers could afford to sell cigars for just five cents. The women making them had quotas that were almost impossible for any human to meet.

While white women were almost always treated better than black or Latina women, business owners still had a pecking order wherein some ethnic groups were considered more desirable than others. In the Lawrence Worsted Mills in Massachusetts, a man of British descent could expect up to $11 a week in wages. In contrast, a woman of German descent would be paid $9 a week for the same job. Her coworkers from Southern Italy doing the same job could only expect to make about $6 a week.

Regardless of race, people who were perceived as different were feared. White people feared that black people and Asian immigrants would take their jobs. That fear metastasized in America, across the north and south. The Klu Klux Klan strengthened its hold and targeted black people through violence. Jim Crow laws—laws that enforced segregation—prevented many black people from fighting a system that was designed to keep them down.

BORN TO WORK

It wasn't just racism and sexism that kept working-class people in factories, on farms, or in homes as domestic servants. The idea that black people were okay living on table scraps, or that Jewish immigrants were satisfied with unsafe working conditions, were symptoms of a larger cultural problem—one that fostered even more discrimination. That problem was a belief that was (and still is) wrapped up in the notion of the American Dream.

Folded into the idea of the American Dream is the assumption that anybody can become successful, as long as they want it bad enough and work hard enough. The truth is—and this is a tough truth to swallow—lots of people work hard their whole lives and still never get there. That's because hard work alone isn't a surefire way to success. People just believed it was. In reality the system was rigged. It was set up to benefit people who already had the most money and controlled the means of production. The Triangle Shirtwaist Factory and others like it existed because immigrants worked hard to survive, but no matter how hard they worked, very few of them were ever going to climb into a new social station. That's because the entire system was set up to reward those who already had money and power! The American Dream made a certain group of people—mostly white people born of a certain class from certain backgrounds—even wealthier than they already were. It was a good deal for them. But not for those who didn't start with the same advantages.

UNEARNED PRIVILEGE

People with advantages started to believe they had earned them, that they were somehow superior to workers. One of the Triangle jurors (on the all-male jury) summed up what many people thought of working immigrant girls: "I think that the girls, who undoubtedly have not as much intelligence as others might have in other walks of life, were inclined to fly into a panic." This statement is plainly ignorant. First of all, panic is a human emotion, not limited to any social class. Second, it is completely unfair to assume the factory girls weren't intelligent based on their gender or proficiency in English. After all, they weren't working in factories because they couldn't cut it in medical school; they were there because their families needed them to contribute to the survival of the family.

Unfortunately, many Americans believed that if a young girl was working in a factory, it was because she was morally suspect. *The New York Times* ran an editorial in 1906 that didn't mince any words: "A nice girl…is not thinking about spending her life in commercial employment." Such a statement reeks of privilege. Only someone who

The Asch Building on the day of the Triangle fire.

has a choice about how he spends his working life would ever utter something so ridiculously ignorant. For millions of Americans, factory life was not a choice. It was a requirement.

Meanwhile, as factory workers struggled to get by, the shirtwaist industry took in $50 million a year. That's over a billion dollars today. That money went to a select few people, mostly white men who came from wealthy or solidly upper-middle-class families. They had advantages that immigrants didn't, but most simply refused to recognize that important fact.

The American Dream does exist for some people. And hard work is important; it's just not the only ingredient for success. Until we as a culture recognize that fact, we are doomed to dismiss the factory girls as nothing more than a tragic footnote in history. What a disservice that is to them! The factory girls helped build our economy, and many died in the process. They didn't work in factories because they were stupid or lazy or unimaginative. They worked to survive.

Triangle worker Pauline Newman put it best when asked how she survived that life: "What alternative did you have? You stayed and you survived, that's all."

CHAPTER 11

HISTORY REPEATS

I am, somehow, less interested in the weight and convolutions of Einstein's brain than in the near certainty that people of equal talent have lived and died in cotton fields and sweatshops.

—Stephen Jay Gould

The Triangle fire happened because of a cigarette. That's the simple answer to what caused such a horrific event. The far more complicated answer is that Americans made a series of choices about labor, production, workplace safety, immigration, fashion, consumerism, and economics. Sometimes those choices were small, so small that Americans didn't know they were making a choice at all. But all those choices led to the conditions inside the Triangle Shirtwaist Factory on March 25, 1911.

The factory girls were the victims of a fire started by a careless smoker, but they were also victims of Gilded Age thinking. The Gilded Age was a period of runaway wealth and greed, a period where getting ahead by stepping on the little guy's neck wasn't just encouraged but expected. Part of that Gilded Age ideology was an entrenched cultural idea that labor was expendable. Factory girls were treated as disposable resources. When one girl left—due to injury or illness or death—the factory owners found another girl to replace her. Someone who might very well accept an even lower wage. The Gilded Age gave rise to an America where greed ruled, no matter what the costs to others.

All our lives, we've been taught to respect our country and revere the people who built it. But you don't have to give up a single ounce of your patriotism to recognize when America is in the wrong. We have much to be proud of, but we have to be honest with ourselves about aspects of our history that aren't so virtuous. While we Americans love to talk about the American Dream—the promise that all citizens, with the right amount of pluck and hard work, can be anything they want—we are often quick to forget about the very people on whose backs the American Dream was built. Factory owners in the early twentieth century may have worked very hard. Many came from modest roots and found ways to build businesses that thrived. But many of those same businessmen (and they were men) succeeded precisely because they were willing to exploit their workers.

Gilded Age thinking is pernicious and is still deeply rooted in American institutions. While the American workplace is undoubtedly safer and more equitable for certain people, we haven't made as much progress as we should have. Unsafe and exploitative working conditions in garment production still exist—and in some places are as bad or worse than those in the Triangle Factory.

OUTSOURCING TRAGEDY

So what is this company, this mass-producing behemoth that's exploiting its workers? Well, the answer is complicated, because it's not just one factory. It's many, many factories. Chances are good that you are wearing something right now that came from one of these factories. The truth is that factories outside the United States, mostly in Asia, now mass-produce cheap clothing that is then sold to Americans like you and me. We are very likely supporting labor and economic policies that are not just similar to those that were common in the early 1900s. They are exactly the same—or even worse!

Factories outside the United States are the new Triangle. Bad policies that privilege profit over safety have simply moved abroad. While we may all agree that American workers deserve rights, we may be unwittingly treating Asian factory workers as expendable because they are invisible to us. We consumers must take some responsibility for that. Even if the United States doesn't directly own or operate those factories, we are part of the problem if we buy materials or completed clothing from factories that practice Triangle-style exploitation of workers.

TRAGEDY IN BANGLADESH

On Saturday, November 25, 2012—101 years after the Triangle fire—a garment factory in Dhaka, Bangladesh, burned to the ground. The factory, called Tazreen Fashions, was housed in a nine-story building where approximately 1,500 people worked on any given day. Just like at the Triangle Factory, Tazreen Fashions employed mostly young women who worked long hours to produce garments. The factory specialized in shirts and fleeces that it supplied to brands around the world, including Wal-Mart, the Gap, and Tommy Hilfiger. And like the Triangle workers, the Tazreen employees were paid paltry wages to work long hours in an unsafe building with few exits, limited fire escapes, and no proper emergency training.

The fire broke out around 7 p.m. in a warehouse where yarn was stored. Within minutes, the building was an inferno. The fire might have been extinguished sooner, but firefighters had difficulty getting to the fire because the road surrounding the factory was too degraded to navigate. While firefighters struggled to get close, the fire wreaked havoc. By the next morning, the death toll was 111 people. It might have been even higher, but more than half of the workers had left before the fire started. The six hundred workers who were still in the factory at 7 p.m. were there because they were working overtime to complete an order.

The cause of the fire is not clear, but officials determined that it was likely started by an electrical problem—or by a cigarette. Like Triangle, Tazreen Fashions had been reported for safety violations in the past, but the owners ordered continued production without making changes to address safety issues. (An inspector from Wal-Mart had cited the factory for safety violations the year before. Wal-Mart allowed factories up to three notices in two years before the company pulled its business for a year. Though Wal-Mart did ultimately pull its business, stores ended up with Tazreen products anyway. That's because the company Wal-Mart hired outsourced its work to a subcontractor who then subcontracted to someone else, and so on. Eventually, the subcontractor was none other than Tazreen.) When the fire happened in 2012, it was hardly a surprise.

Factory fires in Bangladesh are all too common. Between 2006 and 2012, five hundred workers in Bangladesh lost their lives in workplace fires. As the second-largest exporter of garments (second only to China), Bangladesh produces $18 billion worth of clothing every year, employing four million Bangladeshis, mostly women and many children. Regulating factories in this booming business environment is simply not a priority. Just like American factories in the early 1900s, the Bangladeshi factory owners are making money hand over fist and paying the country's garment workers a paltry minimum wage. At the time of the Tazreen fire, that wage was the American equivalent of $37 a month. In 2013 the Bangladeshi government raised the minimum wage to about 5,300 Bangladeshi taka per month, the equivalent of $68 in the United States. That might seem like a lot until you realize that a combo meal at McDonald's is 450 taka. For one month, basic apartment utilities, including electricity and water, run about 2,700 taka; rent for a one-bedroom apartment is close to 10,000. Though the country did take steps to improve wages, you can see how 5,300 taka a month is still not a living wage.

Union organizers attempted to make changes in Bangladeshi factories both before and after the Tazreen fire. But much like American union advocates in the 1900s, Bangladeshi union supporters are facing major obstacles. Factory owners in general are opposed to unions because they want to cut corners (even at the expense of workers) to make more money. Bangladeshis even have a name for this type of factory owner: cowboy operator. Cowboy operators don't play by any rules. They do what they have to do in order to maximize profit, including treating workers as expendable resources.

DISASTER AGAIN

Tragedy struck in Bangladesh once again on Wednesday, April 24, 2013. Rana Plaza, an eight-story building that was home to five garment factories, collapsed. Located twenty miles outside Dhaka, the building was occupied on any given day by some two thousand workers. On April 24, the building collapsed, trapping workers in a pile of rubble. When rescue operations were finally completed, days after the collapse, the death toll stood at 1,135 people.

The Rana Plaza collapse was preventable; the owners had been warned about safety problems when cracks in the building's walls and foundation were spotted. It was later revealed that the building may have been doomed from the outset. To start, the builders didn't have proper permits. The structure was constructed on a swampy pond, making for a spongy foundation. On top of that, the building wasn't sound. After the collapse, one official noted that it was all cement and sand with not enough iron to hold the structure upright. Furthermore, the owner didn't take into consideration the weight of all the equipment placed inside the building. But the owner did nothing to protect his workers. Instead, he chose to cut costs and take his chances with an unsafe building.

The Rana Plaza disaster—one of the largest workplace tragedies in history—reminded the world that what we buy matters. The factories within the building produced garments for multiple worldwide stores and brands, including Benneton, Joe Fresh (distributed by JC Penney), and Wal-Mart. Some sources suggest that major retailers like Wal-Mart had not bought garments from the Rana Plaza companies after the owner was officially warned about possible safety problems. Even so, garments produced at the lowest possible cost in Bangladesh are still being sold at bottom-dollar prices all over the Western world, including in Britain and the United States.

Chances are you've purchased garments that came from unsafe factories in Bangladesh or China—clothes produced cheaply, by underpaid foreign workers, some of whom were very probably children. Our desire for cheap, even disposable, clothes is the fuel that keeps these factories going. Cheap jeans may feel like a fashion find, but they might very well be the thing that is oppressing workers in other countries.

WHAT YOU CAN DO

American factory girls didn't have much of a chance to change American policies on labor and safety because they were completely disenfranchised. They couldn't vote, and they had limited avenues for social, economic, or political influence. Political machines cared little for their interests, and with little extra income—save for a few dollars here and there for a shirtwaist, a movie, or a few sweets—factory girls couldn't put their money to work on their own behalf either. But as a group—a mobilized force—they wielded enormous power, with or without a vote. Even with the deck stacked against them in every way, factory girls fought back. They did something. And they changed the world. It didn't happen overnight. The road was full of roadblocks and detours. Many of the girls wouldn't live to see reform; nor would they live to see all women get the right to vote just a few years after the Triangle fire. But America did change in the era of progressive reform. We as a country agreed that worker exploitation was wrong—a belief that most of us still carry with us today, I hope!

You don't have to be a factory girl to change the world. You don't have to be rich or powerful to change the conditions in overseas factories. You can continue the work that the Triangle girls started. Begin by doing your research. Find out more about where your clothes come from and how they are produced. Lots of websites will help you locate factories that produce garments in safer conditions with better employee wages. Here are some of them:

- The Clean Clothes Campaign (https://cleanclothes.org) is a great resource that helps consumers find "clean" clothes, or clothes that have been produced in factories that pay workers living wages, monitor working conditions, adopt a code of ethical conduct, and allow workers a voice through unions and collective bargaining. In short, the Clean Clothes Campaign seeks to empower workers by helping consumers make better choices.

- Shop Ethical! (http://www.ethical.org.au) is an Australian website that allows you to search for worldwide brands and retailers with records on their treatment of employees.

- The Ethical Fashion Forum (http://www.ethicalfashionforum.com/source-directory) provides a database of ethically sourced products, including clothing, listed by brand. (You'll be surprised how many of your favorite brands don't make the cut.)

- The Good Shopping Guide (http://www.thegoodshopping-guide.com/) presents ratings on multiple brands based on an index of labor policies and fair trade standards. The guides allow you to compare brands.

- The Institute for Global Labour and Human Rights (http://www.globallabourrights.org/) posts reports from all the over world about labor violations. Reading those reports and keeping up with the news related to international labor and production are good ways to know which American brands and retailers are using child labor and/or mistreating their workers.

DON'T GET DISCOURAGED

While you can make small changes with the help of these websites, I'm not going to lie to you: It's really hard to find affordable clothes that you can feel good about. That's because many companies either don't know where their garments are sourced or don't want to know. Or even worse: They don't want you to know. Even companies with the best of intentions have to constantly monitor factories to make sure they are providing safe working conditions, fair pay, and collective bargaining. It's hard to know whom to trust. Even a company with the best of intentions might think it's buying clothes from ethical factories when that's no longer the case.

Even if we stand together and force our favorite brands and retailers to inspect their foreign factories, we have to be sure that it isn't just theater. For instance, factory workers and owners in developing countries have openly talked about all the ways they can avoid being written up by auditors. A Chinese factory, for instance, played a particular song over the loudspeaker when the inspectors arrived in order to signal to all the children to leave by the back door. Factories inspected by Nike, one of the brands most determined to show the world a commitment to ethical production, were not much safer after years of inspection. Some of the factories had gotten even worse. And as we saw with Wal-Mart, subcontracting can make it almost impossible for companies to know where their products are coming from.

You might think that the best solution is to just stop buying clothes. That's certainly one option, and it doesn't mean you can't be fashionable. You can still shop. Just do it in secondhand stores and consignment shops. Make a commitment to recycle your old clothes by donating and consigning. But you still have to be careful because if you stop buying altogether from stores that buy cheap factory-made clothes and sell them for just a few bucks, you may be contributing to factory closures and job losses abroad. That's not good either, given that garment factories employ millions of women. See what I mean? This is a really complicated issue that requires a thoughtful approach.

STAY VIGILANT

So besides boycotting, what else can we do? Well, some experts believe that factories in developing countries have to reach a point where unfair labor practices (including child labor) are simply not culturally acceptable. But that's a tough pill to swallow when people are suffering and even dying as a result of current labor practices.

On our end, we have to be very careful that we don't absolve ourselves and believe that we can buy anything we want while we wait for countries in the developing world to change their attitudes about labor. Instead, we have to agree together—as consumers and producers—that how we treat workers matters to who we are as human beings. We have to agree that while solutions are not easy to find, we have to keep talking about the issue. We have to agree that policies matter.

In that spirit, here are three things you can do right now, even if you aren't old enough to vote, to ensure that the world doesn't forget the world's most vulnerable laborers.

- Learn. The old adage is true: When we don't understand history, we are bound to repeat it. Read about labor in America. (You can find a list in For Further Reading at the end of the book.) Read newspapers. Read articles about labor and economic policies. Educate yourself about the past, and prepare yourself for the future.

- Talk. Tell your friends, your parents, your teachers, or anyone else who wants to talk with you about what you are learning. Ask for other people's opinions. Share what you've learned. Keep the issue in the open. Talking about it means you are on the road to making more informed decisions.

- Listen. If you keep your ears open, you'll hear all kinds of things. You'll hear some politicians complaining about regulations in America. Listen carefully to what they're saying. Do they want to eliminate regulations to increase the profits of a few while leaving workers even more vulnerable to potential abuses? Do they want to eliminate regulations that would make working conditions worse for those workers overseas? Do they sympathize with companies who seek to eliminate avenues for workers to legally unionize and fairly bargain? Do they talk about workers as expendable resources? Listen carefully. Then respond. You have power, but only if you know the facts. Don't be like the Gilded Age Americans who allowed greed and corruption to predominate.

Once upon a time Americans lived in a country where girls were locked in factories and made to work without adequate pay and without any guarantee of their safety or well being. That time in America is largely gone. That's in no small part because of the Triangle girls. We owe them a debt. We owe it to them to keep this issue alive. We can do that by being educated citizens who care deeply about how others are treated, and by being ever vigilant against the malignant forces of greed. We must remember the Triangle girls by remembering what they did to change the world.

FOR FURTHER READING

Andrew Brooks. *Clothing Poverty: The Hidden World of Fast Fashion and Second-Hand Clothes.* London: Zed Books, 2015.

> Think secondhand clothes are the answer to the problem of fast fashion? Think again. Brooks explores the problems associated with thrift and charity stores.

Elizabeth L. Cline. *The Shockingly High Cost of Cheap Fashion.* New York: Portfolio, 2012.

> You might be giddy when you find a screaming good deal on clothes, but the reality is that whoever made that item of super cheap clothing probably didn't get paid much in order to give you that deal. Cline suggests alternatives for fashion, including refashioning older styles and sewing your own clothes.

Barbara Ehrenreich. *Nickel and Dimed. On (Not) Getting By in America.* 10th Anniversary Edition. New York: Picador, 2011.

> If you think it's easy to live on minimum wage, think again. Ehrenreich set out to try it by working at different low-wage jobs, including hotel cleaner, house cleaner, nursing home aide, waitress, and Wal-mart clerk. She demonstrates the toll that bad jobs and low wages takes on workers.

Susan A. Glenn. *Daughters of the Shtetl: Life and Labor in the Immigrant Generation.* Ithaca, NY: Cornell University Press, 1990.

> Eastern European immigrants came to America to live better lives, but they often suffered extreme discrimination. Glenn's book tells the story of Jewish women whose labor built the garment industry.

Albert Marrin. *Flesh and Blood So Cheap: The Triangle Fire and Its Legacy.* New York: Alfred A. Knopf, 2011.

Filled with photos and illustrations, Marrin's book transports you to the Triangle Factory on that fateful day in 1911. The book brings the factory to life.

Priscilla Murolo and A. B. Chitty. *From the Folks Who Brought You the Weekend: A Short, Illustrated History of Labor in the United States*. New York: The New Press, 2012.

How we think about labor in America is a relatively recent phenomenon. We connect work with moral goodness. Yet Murolo and Chitty point out that such an ideology makes it easy for industries to exploit us. Learn about how our ideas about labor have shifted and changed over history.

Leon Stein. *The Triangle Fire*. Ithaca, New York: Cornell University Press, 1962.

Stein provides the definitive book on the Triangle fire. Filled with quotes and oral histories of survivors, it reminds readers that hundreds of real people were affected by the fire.

David von Drehle. *Triangle: The Fire That Changed America*. New York: Grove Press, 2003.

Von Drehle's book covers much of the same ground that Stein's book does, but he goes an extra step to talk about the way the world changed after the fire. After the fire, American ideas about work, labor, and safety changed significantly for the better.

Barbara Mayer Wertheimer. *We Were There: The Story of Working Women in America*. New York: Random House, 1977.

Throughout history, women have done all the same jobs as men. They've just done them for less pay and less respect, and often in less safe conditions. Learn about the women who changed our world, but who haven't always gotten credit for doing so.

SELECTED REFERENCES

"141 Men and Girls Die in Waist Factory Fire." *New York Times,* March 26, 1911, New York Times Archives, http://graphics8.nytimes.com/packages/pdf/archives/waistcoatfire-03-26-1911.pdf.

"1890s Shirtwaist." FIDM Museum and Galleries. http://blog.fidmmuseum.org/museum/2010/09/1890s-shirtwaist.html.

"2014 Characteristics of New Housing." US Department of Commerce. https://www.census.gov/construction/chars/pdf/c25ann2014.pdf.

Ackerman, S. J. "The Vote That Failed." *Smithsonian,* November 1998, http://www.smithsonianmag.com/history/the-vote-that-failed-159427766/?no-ist.

Al-Mahmood, Syed Zain. "Nexus of Politics, Corruption Doomed Rana Plaza." *Dhaka Tribune,* April 26, 2013, http://archive.dhakatribune.com/politics/2013/apr/26/nexus-politics-corruption-doomed-rana-plaza.

"Austro-Hungarian Immigration." Immigrant Groups. *Immigration to North America,* http://immigrationtous.net/28-austro-hungarian-immigration.html.

Bajaj, Vikas. "Fatal Fire in Bangladesh Highlights the Dangers Facing Garment Workers." *New York Times,* Nov. 25, 2012, http://www.nytimes.com/2012/11/26/world/asia/bangladesh-fire-kills-more-than-100-and-injures-many.html.

Barrett, Nancy J. "The Struggles of Women Industrial Workers to Improve Work Conditions in the Progressive Era." *OAH Magazine of History,* vol. 13, no. 3, 1999, pp. 43–49.

"Bessie Cohen." *Toledo Blade,* Feb. 24, 1999, https://news.google.com/newspapers?nid=1350&dat=19990224&id=7kBPAAAAIBAJ&sjid=mwMEAAAAIBAJ&pg=4447,3166348&hl=en "Biography: Anne Morgan." *American Experience: Triangle Fire,* http://www.pbs.org/wgbh/americanexperience/features/biography/triangle-morgan/.

"Biography: Clara Lemlich." *American Experience: Triangle Fire,* http://www.pbs.org/wgbh/americanexperience/features/biography/triangle-lemlich/.

"Biography: Pauline Newman." *American Experience: Triangle Fire,* http://www.pbs.org/wgbh/americanexperience/features/biography/triangle-newman/.

Blakemore, Erin. "The Gibson Girls: The Kardashians of the Early 1900s." *Mental Floss*, Sept. 17, 2014, http://mentalfloss.com/article/58591/gibson-girls-kardashians-early-1900s.

Blanke, David. *The 1910s. American Popular Culture Through History.* Westport, CT: Greenwood Press, 2002.

Boyd, Andrew. "No. 2683: Taylorism." *Engines of our Ingenuity,* www.uh.edu/engines/epi2683/htm.

Brands, H. W. *American Colussus: The Triumph of Capitalism, 1865–1900.* Doubleday, 2010.

Brooks, Andrew. *Clothing Poverty: The Hidden World of Fast Fashion and Second-Hand Clothes.* London: Zed Books, 2015

Burke, Edmund. "Letter to the Sheriffs of Bristol." *The Works of the Right Hon. Edmund Burke.* London: Holdsworth and Ball, 1834. Google Book Search.

Burt, Elizabeth V. "Working Women and the Triangle Fire: Press Coverage of a Tragedy." *Journalism History*, 30: 4 (Winter 2005), pp. 189–199.

Carnegie, Andrew. "Wealth." *North American Review,* June 1889, Swarthmore College, https://www.swarthmore.edu/SocSci/rbannis1/AIH19th/Carnegie.html.

Chazanov, Mathis. "Fire Haunts 93-year-old: Survivor of 1911 Triangle Factory Blaze Tries to Forget." *Los Angeles Times*, March 17, 1985, http://articles.latimes.com/1985-03-17/news/we-35678_1_triangle-fire.

"Clayton Anti-Trust Act." *Encyclopaedia Britannica,* https://www.britannica.com/event/Clayton-Antitrust-Act.

Dash, Joan. *We Shall Not Be Moved: The Women's Factory Strike of 1909.* New York: Scholastic, 1995.

"Death List is 141; Only 86 Identified." *New York Times*, March 27, 1911, *American Experience,* http://www.pbs.org/wgbh/americanexperience/features/primary-resources/triangle-death-list/.

Duhigg, Charles. *Smarter, Faster, Better: The Secrets of Being Productive in Life and Business.* New York: Random House, 2016.

Ehrenreich, Barbara. *Nickel and Dimed. On (Not) Getting By in America.* 10th Anniversary Edition. New York: Picador, 2011.

"Ellis Island." *New York Harbor Parks,* http://www.nyharborparks.org/visit/elis-faq.html.

"Ellis Island History." *The Statue of Liberty*, Ellis Island Foundation, Inc., http://www.libertyellisfoundation.org/ellis-island-history#1907.

Emerson, Ralph Waldo. "Essay VII: Politics." *Ralph Waldo Emerson Texts*. Emerson Central. http://www.emersoncentral.com/politics.htm.

Fitzgerald, F. Scott. *The Great Gatsby*. 39th ed. New York: Scribners, 2003.

Freeman, Joshua. "Remembering the Triangle Fire." *The Nation*, March 16, 2011, https://www.thenation.com/article/remembering-triangle-fire/.

Frowne, Sadie. "Days and Dreams." *Remembering the 1911 Triangle Factory Fire*, Cornell University, http://trianglefire.ilr.cornell.edu/primary/testimonials/ootss_sadiefrowne.html.

"The Gilded Age Billionaires, Part 1." *New York Social Diary*, Aug. 8, 2006, http://www.newyorksocialdiary.com/social-history/2006/the-gilded-age-billionaires-part-i.

"The Girl on the Swing." *History of Criminal Justice*, Illinois State University, http://my.ilstu.edu/~ftmorn/cjhistory/casestud/shaw.html.

"Girls Risked Lives in Order to Save Others in Peril." *New York Evening Telegram,* March 27, 1911, Remember the Triangle Fire Coalition, http://rememberthetrianglefire.org/open-archive/wp-content/uploads/2011/03/NY-Eve-Tel-Crop.pdf.

Glenn, Susan A. *Daughters of the Shtetl: Life and Labor in the Immigrant Generation*. Ithaca, NY: Cornell University Press, 1990.

"Glossary on the Eleanor Roosevelt Papers Project: Tammany Hall." *Teaching Eleanor Roosevelt*, https://www.gwu.edu/~erpapers/teachinger/glossary/tammany-hall.cfm.

Gompers, Samuel. "Eight Hours: The Workers and the Eight-hour Workday and the Shorter Workday, and Its Philosophy." The American Federation of Labor, *Archive.org*, https://archive.org/stream/eighthoursworker00gomp/eighthoursworker00gomp_djvu.txt.

Gould, Stephen Jay. *The Panda's Thumb: More Reflections in Natural History*. New York: Norton, 1980.

Hammond, Claudia. "Is Reading in the Dark Bad for Your Eyesight?" *Future*, BBC. Oct. 2, 2012, http://www.bbc.com/future/story/20121001-should-you-read-in-the-dark.

Herzberg, Frederick; Mausner, Bernard; and Snyderman, Barbara B. *The Motivation to Work*. 2nd ed. New York: John Wiley, 1959.

Hobbes, Michael. "The Myth of the Ethical Shopper." *Highline. The Huffington Post*, http://highline.huffingtonpost.com/articles/en/the-myth-of-the-ethical-shopper/.

Holste, Glenda. "If Bodies Fell From Today's City, Would Anyone Hear Them?" *St. Paul Pioneer Press*, Feb. 26, 1999, *LexisNexis*.

Husock, Howard. "The Bangladesh Disaster and Corporate Social Responsibility." *Forbes*, May 2, 2013, http://www.forbes.com/sites/howardhusock/2013/05/02/the-bangladesh-fire-and-corporate-social-responsibility/#2dd3cbdc55fe.

"Immigrants in the Progressive Era." *Progressive Era to New Era, 1900-1929*, Library of Congress, http://www.loc.gov/teachers/classroommaterials/presentationsandactivities/presentations/timeline/progress/immigrnt/.

"Immigration in the Early 1900s." *Immigration in the Early Twentieth Century, Eyewitness to History*, http://www.eyewitnesstohistory.com/snpim1.htm.

Ingersoll, Robert G. "About Farming in Illinois." *The Works of Robert G. Ingersoll*. New York: Cosimo, 1900. Google Book Search.

Jennifer. "Kate Leone." *Find a Grave*, May 18, 2005, http://www.findagrave.com/cgi-bin/fg.cgi?page=gr&GRid=10987235.

Jensen, Robin E.; Doss, Erin F.; and Ivic, Rebecca. "Metaphorical Invention in Early Photojournalism: *New York Times Coverage* of the 1876 Brooklyn Theater Fire and the 1911 Shirtwaist Factory Fire." *Critical Studies in Media Communication*, 28:4, October 2011, pp. 334–352.

Kaplan, Justin. *When the Astors Owned New York: Blue Bloods and Grand Hotels*. New York: Viking, 2006.

Kaufman, Michael T. "Bessie Cohen, 107, Survivor Of 1911 Shirtwaist Fire, Dies." *New York Times*, Feb. 24, 1999, http://www.nytimes.com/1999/02/24/nyregion/bessie-cohen-107-survivor-of-1911-shirtwaist-fire-dies.html.

Kennedy, Robert C. "On This Day: September 30, 1893." *New York Times*, The Learning Network, https://www.nytimes.com/learning/general/onthisday/harp/0930.html.

Ladies Garment Worker. April 1911. *Remembering the 1911 Triangle Factory Fire*, Cornell University, http://trianglefire.ilr.cornell.edu/primary/newspapersmagazines/lgw_0411.html.

Lansner, Jonathan. "Lansner and His Great Aunt Fannie: Did We Forget Triangle Fire's Lessons?" *The Orange County Register*, March 21, 2015, http://

www.ocregister.com/articles/workers-655050-fannie-american.html

Lansner, Jonathan. "Lessons from 146 Dead Workers 100 Years Ago." *The Orange County Register*, March 25, 2011, http://www.ocregister.com/articles/-292646--.html.

Lazarus, Emma. "The New Colossus." *Statue of Liberty*, National Park Service, https://www.nps.gov/stli/learn/historyculture/colossus.htm.

Lears, Jackson. *Rebirth of a Nation: The Making of Modern America, 1877–1920*. New York: Harper Perennial, 2010.

Lepore, Jill. "Away From My Desk: The Office From Beginning to End." *The New Yorker*, May 12, 2014, http://www.newyorker.com/magazine/2014/05/12/away-from-my-desk.

Lichtenstein, Nelson. *Walter Reuther: The Most Dangerous Man in Detroit*. Urbana, IL: University of Illinois Press, 1995. Google Book Search.

Linder, Doug. "The Triangle Shirtwaist Factory Fire Trial." *Famous Trials*, University of Missouri–Kansas City, 2002, http://law2.umkc.edu/faculty/projects/ftrials/triangle/triangleaccount.html.

Lincoln, Abraham. "Speech in New Haven, Connecticut." *Vindicating the Founders*, http://www.vindicatingthefounders.com/library/new-haven-speech.html.

Marrin, Albert. *Flesh and Blood So Cheap: The Triangle Fire and Its Legacy*. New York: Alfred A. Knopf, 2011.

Martin, Douglas. "Rose Freedman, Last Survivor of Triangle Fire, Dies at 107." *New York Times*, Feb. 17, 2001, http://www.nytimes.com/2001/02/17/nyregion/rose-freedman-last-survivor-of-triangle-fire-dies-at-107.html?pagewanted=all.

Martin, Frederick Townsend. *The Passing of the Idle Rich*. Garden City, NY: Doubleday, 1911. Archive.org Search. https://archive.org/stream/passingofidleric00martiala/passingofidleric00martiala_djvu.txt.

McCracken, Elizabeth. "The Lives They Lived: Rose Freedman, B. 1893; Out of the Fire." *New York Times*, Dec. 30, 2001, http://www.nytimes.com/2001/12/30/magazine/the-lives-they-lived-rose-freedman-b-1893-out-of-the-fire.html.

Mee, John F. "Frederick W. Taylor." *Encyclopaedia Britannica*, https://www.britannica.com/biography/Frederick-W-Taylor.

Moore, Tony. "Boss Tweed Biography." *Biography.com*, http://www.biography.com/people/boss-tweed-20967991.

"Mourning & Protest, Victims & Survivors**."** *Remembering the 1911 Triangle Factory Fire*, Cornell University, http://trianglefire.ilr.cornell.edu/primary/photosillustrations/slideshow.html?image_id=897&sec_id=6.

Murolo, Priscilla, and Chitty, A. B. *From the Folks Who Brought You the Weekend: A Short, Illustrated History of Labor in the United States*. New York: The New Press, 2012.

Mustafa, Sabir. "Dhaka Factory Collapse: Can Clothes Industry Change?" *BBC News*. Apr. 25, 2013, http://www.bbc.com/news/world-asia-22302595.

"The Name that Launched a Million Bottles." The Annette and Irwin Eskind Biomedical Library, Vanderbilt University, http://www.mc.vanderbilt.edu/diglib/sc_diglib/hc/nostrums/pinkham.html.

Nawaz, A.S.M. Sararez. "Employee Motivation: A Study on Some Selected McDonalds in the UK." *African Journal of Business Management,*. vol. 5, no. 14 (July 2011), pp. 5541–5550.

Newman, Pauline. "Letter to Michael and Hugh From Pauline M. Newman." *Remembering the 1911 Triangle Factory Fire*, Cornell University, http://trianglefire.ilr.cornell.edu/primary/letters/paulinenewman.html.

O'Donnell, Edward T. *America in the Gilded Age and Progressive Era*. The Great Courses, The Teaching Company, 2015.

Oppenheim, James. "Bread and Roses." *Poems for Workers: An Anthology*. The Little Red Library, edited by Manuel Gomez. Chicago: The Daily Worker Publishing Co., 1925, https://www.marxists.org/history/usa/pubs/lrlibrary/05-LRL-poem.pdf.

Orleck, Annelise. *Common Sense and a Little Fire: Women and Working-Class Politics in the United States, 1900-1965 (Gender and American Culture)*. Chapel Hill, NC: University of North Carolina Press, 1995.

Papers and Proceedings of the Seventeenth General Meeting of the American Library Association. American Library Association, 1895, Google Book Search.

"Passenger List." *The Statue of Liberty*. Ellis Island Foundation, Inc., http://libertyellisfoundation.org/passenger.

Rana Plaza Collapse: 38 Charged with Murder Over Garment Factory Disaster." *The Guardian*, July 18, 2016, https://www.theguardian.com/world/2016/jul/18/rana-plaza-collapse-murder-charges-garment-factory.

Reese, Ashley. "11 Of Your Favorite Clothing Brands That Use Sweatshop Labor." *Gurl.* May 1, 2016, http://www.gurl.com/2016/05/01/clothing-stores-and-brands-that-use-sweatshop-labor/#ixzz4Pf6HwwTM.

Roosevelt, Franklin Delano. "One Third of a Nation." FDR's Second Inaugural Address. *History Matters*, George Mason University, http://historymatters.gmu.edu/d/5105/.

Roucek, Joseph S. "The Image of the Slave in U.S. History and in Immigration Policy." *American Journal of Economics and Sociology*, vol. 28, no. 1 (January 1969), pp. 29–48.

"Saks & Company." Advertisement. *New York Times*, March 26, 1911, *LexisNexis*.

San Ethirajan, Anbara. "Dhaka Building Collapse: Dozens Found Alive in Rubble." *BBC News*, April 25, 2013, http://www.bbc.com/news/world-asia-22299929.

Serratore, Angela. "How American Rich Kids Bought Their Way into the British Elite." *The Smithsonian*, Aug. 13, 2013, http://www.smithsonianmag.com/ist/?next=/history/how-american-rich-kids-bought-their-way-into-the-british-elite-4252/.

Stein, Leon. *The Triangle Fire*. Ithaca, NY: Cornell University Press, 1962.

"The Story of Sadie Frowne, A Brooklyn Sweatshop Girl." Herb Social History for Every Classroom, *American Social History Project*, City University of New York, http://herb.ashp.cuny.edu/items/show/891.

Strasser, Susan. "Customer to Consumer: The New Consumption in the Progressive Era." *OAH Magazine of History*, vol. 13, no. 3 (Spring 1999), pp. 10–14.

"Survivor Oral Histories." *Remembering the 1911 Triangle Factory Fire*, Cornell University, https://trianglefire.ilr.cornell.edu/primary/survivorInterviews/PaulinePepe.html.

"Tammany Hall." *Encyclopaedia Britannica*, https://www.britannica.com/topic/Tammany-Hall.

"Taylorism." *Encyclopaedia Britannica*, https://www.britannica.com/topic/Taylorism.

Trachtenberg, Alan. *The Incorporation of America: Culture & Society in the Gilded Age*. New York: Hill and Wang, 1982.

"Triangle Shirtwaist Factory Fire." *All Things Considered*, March 25, 2001, http://www.npr.org/programs/watc/features/2001/010325.triangle.html.

"Unions and Labor." *Stubby's Labor Quotes*, http://laborquotes.weebly.com/unions--labor.html.

United States Census Bureau. "Annual Estimates of the Resident Population for Incorporated Places of 50,000 or More." *American Fact Finder*, 2015, http://factfinder.census.gov/faces/tableservices/jsf/pages/productview.xhtml?src=bkmk.

"Victim Information." *Remembering the Triangle Fire*. Cornell University, http://trianglefire.ilr.cornell.edu/victimswitnesses/victimDetail.html?victimId=88.

Von Drehle, David. *Triangle: The Fire That Changed America*. New York: Grove Press, 2003.

Washington, George. "From George Washington to Francis Adrian Van der Kemp." May 28, 1788, *Founders Online*, National Archives, https://founders.archives.gov/documents/Washington/04-06-02-0266.

Wertheimer, Barbara Mayer. *We Were There: The Story of Working Women in America*. New York: Random House, 1977.

What Is a Shirtwaist?" *American Experience*, http://www.pbs.org/wgbh/americanexperience/features/general-article/triangle-shirtwaist/.

What Were President Theodore Roosevelt's Accomplishments?" *Inside Gov. by Graphix*, http://us-presidents.insidegov.com/q/16/9699/What-were-President-Theodore-Roosevelt-s-accomplishments.

Woog, Adam. *The 1900s: A Cultural History of the United States Through the Decades*. San Diego, CA: Lucent Books, 1999.

Yardley, Jim. "Bangladesh Takes Steps to Increase Lowest Pay." *New York Times*, Nov. 4, 2013, http://www.nytimes.com/2013/11/05/world/asia/bangladesh-takes-step-toward-raising-38-a-month-minimum-wage.html.

ACKNOWLEDGEMENTS

I owe a truckload of thanks to the many people who helped make this book possible. Everyone at Zest deserves a medal, especially Daniel Harmon. This is a better book because of his thoughtful and careful input. Any mistakes left in the book are now mine alone. Thanks also to Emma Boyer, Adam Grano, and Judith Dunham for their thoughtful work.

Thanks to Alyssa Eisner Henkin at Trident Media Group for being a fierce agent.

The research and writing of Leon Stein and David von Drehle were integral in understanding what happened that day in the factory. Cornell University's ILR School has created a treasure trove of free and easily accessible information, including priceless primary sources, on their Remembering the Triangle Fire website. Anyone who writes about the fire is indebted to them.

Thank you to my students and colleagues at Westminster College who are unfailingly interested in whatever I'm writing and always eager to lend a helping hand. Thanks to Arikka Von, Krista D'Angelis, Autumn Thatcher, Johanna Snow, and Anita Boeira for never getting tired of promoting me and my work on campus and beyond. (Special thanks to Anita for always coming through in a pinch, whether I need a photo, graphic design advice, or a waffle.) Janine Wittwer may in fact be the world's most supportive colleague. Thanks also to Dick Chapman and Curtis Newbold for being unfailingly supportive friends and colleagues. Special thanks to Stephanie Held for brainstorming with me.

I'm lucky to be surrounded by brilliant friends who love books and never tire of thinking aloud with me. Danielle Caldwell has spent hours and hours in conversation with me about writing. I can't think of anyone I'd rather be with in a made-up, two-person MFA program. Katie Palfreyman's love of reading and insightful commentary on absolutely everything continues to delight me. Mandy Anger keeps me sane and never says no to an evening of cheese and treats. Carly Thornton and Amy Kelly have been integral in helping me think through thorny ideas of all kinds. Ashley Seitz Kramer deserves special accolades for being a tireless champion who has given me some of the best writing and life advice I've ever received.

Shout-out to my family for thinking I'm the best, even when I don't deserve it. Bill and Carol Hoverson are truly extraordinary parents. (Thanks, Mom, for sharing your writing with me. You inspire me.) Ken and Jeanette Twelves are like my second set of parents; they are a gift from the universe. Greg Hoverson is aces as a big brother.

Hey, Robert Seifert: Thanks for everything. You are a saint.